FOR NERUDA,
FOR CHILE:
*AN INTERNATIONAL
ANTHOLOGY*

"Tyranny beheads the bards, but by secret
subterranean springs their voice returns from
the bottom of the well to the surface, and even in
the darkness rises to the lips of the people."

—*Pablo Neruda*

"This is how we write the first page of this
history. My people and America will write the
rest."

—*Salvador Allende*

RUDOLF FABRY

What About It, Brother World?

The rulers of the Andes are eagles.
Condors are the kings of Cordilleras,
your predators, Chile, I know so well
via the poems Pablo sang about you,
are murderers.
They strangled your babies in their cradles,
they slashed Liberty's throat . . .

Bow humbly and trembling,
sacrifice yourself like sheep.
Know, as you bleed, at this very moment
an innocent, gentle, pure-white lambkin
was slaughtered.
The lambkin's name: Chile.

What about it, Brother World?
What about it, our planet, Earth?

Translated from the Slovak
by Anča Vrbovská

For Neruda, For Chile

An International Anthology

Edited by Walter Lowenfels

Beacon Press ✤ *Boston*

Beacon Press books are published under the auspices of the Unitarian Universalist Association

Simultaneous publication in Canada by Saunders of Toronto, Ltd.

Published in simultaneous hardcover and paperback editions
Printed in the United States of America

9   8   7   6   5   4   3   2   1

Library of Congress Cataloging in Publication Data

Lowenfels, Walter, 1897–   comp.
    For Neruda, for Chile.
    Includes bibliographical references.
    1. Neruda, Pablo, 1904–1973, in fiction, drama, poetry, etc.   2. Poetry, Modern—20th century.
I. Title.
PN6110.N35L6   808.81'9'351   74-16666
ISBN 0-8070-6382-7
ISBN 0-8070-6383-5 (pbk.)

FROM THE EDITOR

On September 11, 1973, the Popular Unity Government of Chile was overthrown and President Salvador Allende was murdered. A few days afterward, Pablo Neruda died. In the United States from coast to coast, and throughout the world, there were memorial services and read-ins. And many poems were written for Neruda and for Chile. Some of these are brought together here, along with a few eyewitness accounts of events in Chile.

For Neruda, For Chile transcends, I believe, the limits often assigned to poetry. This book speaks not just for the poets in it, but for millions of people who have been moved by the Chilean tragedy.

Furthermore, the reader should know that the book contains only a small selection of the hundreds of poems the editor collected from the five continents.

What's at stake in the book? "The enemy triumphs," Walt Whitman wrote in an introduction to *Leaves of Grass*, "the prison, the handcuffs, the iron necklace and anklet, the scaffold, garrote and leadballs do their work . . . the cause is asleep . . . the strong throats are choked with their own blood . . . the young men drop their eyelashes toward the ground when they pass each other . . . and is liberty gone out of that place? No never. When liberty goes it is not the first to go nor the second or third to go . . . it waits for all the rest to go . . . it is the last . . . when all life and all the souls of men and women are discharged from any part of the earth—then only shall the instinct of liberty be discharged from that part of the earth."

Table of contents and acknowledgments will be found at the end of the book, along with a chronology of Neruda's life and a brief outline of Chilean history.

HORTENSIA BUSSI DE ALLENDE

When in the future, on college campuses and at universities "democracy" is spoken of, and when the case of Chile is discussed, when students and professors see that it was in that tranquil and happy corner of the globe that democracy was assassinated, the sinister figures of international capitalism and its foreign and domestic henchmen will emerge from the shadows. You will recognize them by their bloodstained hands, hands stained by the blood of students, workers, peasants.

Then, my friends, recalling Chile and Salvador Allende, you will recognize the real enemies of the people, my people and your people, and at the same time you will understand the true path that leads to a better society.

From a message by President Allende's widow,
October 15, 1973.

I. Grief Is a Large Space

MARGOT DE SILVA

Don Pablo Neruda

I remember your silence
Like the silence of the *salitre* flats at night
Green under the moon
Drenched in the quietude of *el norte*

I remember your eyes
The slantwise eyes of those
Monsters of the deep
That perceive the stars magnified
By leagues of liquid salt

I remember your skin, Pablo
Tough, yellow as the Cordillera de la Costa
Nourished with your flesh
On the sparse herbs of Araucano

I remember the warmth of your hand
And your voice
That rises from the depths
Like the nasal twang of a steel guitar

I remember your silence
Like the silence of the *salitre* flats at night
Green under the moon
Drenched in the quietude of *el norte*

EVA BAN

In Memoriam Pablo Neruda   (USA—1973)

To the people who took my own country's freedom I owe this poem and the emotion that made me feel Chile's wounds as mine.

When I was sixteen, I knew Pablo Neruda
and heard his voice boom out to the
beaches of Copacabana, heated and
always involved with justice and love.
I saw him string the guitar and
dance samba and make eyes at brown women
and weep for Chile, while I showed him
Brazil, green, lush, full of sunlight, free . . .

And then I grew up and read his verses
and Pablo Neruda was all over the world
and I remembered him while I myself was
stringing words to words, seeking to gather
in a clenched fist sunbursts and passion.
I remembered him.
                    And I thought of him
when soldiers and tanks took over
my country and I understood him in 64
and 65 and 66 when jails were filled with
people and I knew what torture was on my own body . . .
and when he wrote me in veiled lines,
I remembered him and threw the letter away
as prudent warriors do in stressed times;
in Brazil, after nine years
the Generals still reign—can anyone
say that a dictatorship is less worse
than another?
In your country, it is now even worse . . .
At least Rio was not bombed,
books are hidden but not burned . . .
Pablo my friend whom I remember from

4

my girlish past and understand
from the "now"—I weep for us in South
America where Simon Bolívar will rise again
And Anita Garibaldi will ride the pampas
of Brazil anew and your poems shall help
free Chile—
I remember you, Pablo Neruda,
in this country where our South American
blood is used as dividends of big companies
and our tears are but prime materials
for Detroit, cobalt bombs and the making
of weapons then sold to us again
as power to our oppressors . . .
We shout together Chile Brazil Uruguay Paraguay
our day will come
and then you will see! Out of the earth
will come our freedom and we will give
our sorrow double back.

All the lamps
will go out
in this land.

ARAGON

Élégie à Pablo Neruda

an extract

Pablo my friend you were saying in that anguished voice
    Where strange thoughts are made
Only grief is a large space and only blood makes the world
    Wherever I go nothing changes

I know this suffering of all things which mouth their torment
    Bitter like the hawthorn

To all the words to all the cries to all the steps, wanderings
    Where the soul can be glimpsed
Pablo my friend we are the men of this uncertain century
    Where not even the roofs are steady
And on the hill when we think morning is about to break
    It is a distant headlight

We are men of the night who carry the sun within themselves
    It burns into our deepest being
We walked in the dark until we could no longer feel our knees
    Without ever reaching the world to be

Pablo my friend time passes, our voices are already dimming
    Even the heartbeat has faded
Was everything only what had been, what we see now
    Had everything only been a stage
Can one really be satisfied with the color of cruelty
    Where living is at best surviving
Where at best we will have been disenchanted enchanters
    To have sung gold for copper

    Pablo my friend what have we allowed
    The shadow ever lengthens in front of us
    What have we allowed Pablo my friend
    Pablo my friend our dreams our dreams

Translated from the French by
Serge Gavronsky

JOHN TAGLIABUE

The Self Not Seen

Down the corridor the parts of the body
the flowers of the night torn apart

my friend gone
the bleeding hand

from the brain of the dreamer now
animals howling

and the men with machine guns
patrol the almost empty streets

I once sent a poem to you
and we drank wine and laughed looking
at the Pacific

who can silence the revolution
of the surrealist poem

some bleeding towels
are wheeled down the corridor

and the TV flickers
all over the world saying

the Pacific is burning its poems

September 1973

MIGUEL ANGEL ASTURIAS

Pablo Neruda Alive

October of destruction in Guatemala,
betrayal of the *fruiteros*' army,
anguished people
laid their grief on your heart
when the taste of the sky
dried out in their mouths
and a downpour of salt
drenched their faces . . .

You, poet, forever listening
to the suffering of mankind,
you understood in that month of June,
fifty-fourth of the century—
month of seeds and swallows—
the martyrdom of the tropics
when the veins of the *bananales* were slashed . . .

Now
Chile and its people's triumphs
lie under the military heel
scourged by ruin and persecution.
The diastole and systole
of a single heart:
Allende, the diastole,
Neruda, the systole,
and nothing can separate them.
Because of what they did—
no more requiem after requiem
but victory after victory.
The greatness of Chile, pride of the Americas
will rise even higher.
And Neruda's poems like seagulls over spume
will sing beyond a thousand years
beyond time . . .

Now
The conflict continues
in Chile's blood.
Your fate is the spark
that lights us to flame
your poems of fire
will brand the tyrants,
the traitors, the lackeys.

Let no one say you're dead
I declare you alive!
I declare it again:
for when Chile calls
you answer: PRESENT!

Translated from the Spanish by Nan Braymer

RAMONA WEEKS

For Neruda

Why does the wound in the snow gape,
a voiceless mouth
dumbstruck by the glare
that glances deep in the throat
and separates
light from its singing?

What were you that the window
sinks with its own sashweight,
sliding before the high registers
of singing?
Why does memory, singing,
spill over with milk
and pain from the past?

Winter-garrotted, the porcelain jar
lifts its mouth from the snow.
We vainly listen for dumb music
to rise, to roar across the isthmus
that is a green canal between oceans.

We will pass from one to the other,
lifted like cargo, roped with memory,
set ashore on white wharves
to remember.

The stickleback of Tierra del Fuego
howls in the high storms,
and the white spine of the world
cracks: a jereboam flash
where the bones knit and open
for the last time
instead of the voice and the heart:
showing cordilleras of leaves,
leaving the voice and the window
sliding: a glass coffin for insurgent memories
rising: the lover of chinas poblanas
and heavens singing surely,
with the certain lisp
of a lover.

MICHAEL GIZZI

For & After Pablo Neruda

death
was your other pocket
the dark room
where you kept
the negative
of your hand

your moon sulks
in an empty shoe
I hear the shuffle
of your soul
your feet
beneath the flesh
like a thing
begun in sorrow
& the wind bangs
the heart back

Pablo—
they have killed you
& called it nature
they have ordered
all the stones
upon your grave
to keep you still

Pablo—
death is a caravan
it knows its outriders
like a pocket
only the hand remembers

RAFAEL ALBERTI

With Pablo Neruda in My Heart

an extract

. . . Pablo Neruda died. (I heard it in the early morning hours.)
They corrected the news, although it did not matter.
It is through my tears that I now remember these things.

How could I forget that morning on the roof of my house,
the last snow whitening the blue background of the Guadarrama
    mountains,

11

the first words of our meeting,
his distant image becoming presence at last?
You gave us everything then,
your sweetness of a brother newly arrived,
your desolate songs like rivers
and we gave you our joy
and in return we offered our hands which you were long expecting,
and thus your vast solitude was populated,
and it was Miguel and it was Manolo, Vicente, Federico . . .
it was the lyrical voice of Spain
riding the wings of your green horse
because the winds he cut were beautiful
and beautiful were the echoes of its hooves on the worn stone.
But one day the face of Spain was bathed in blood,
her old heart was cut by a knife,
a flood of hatred gushed out of the darkness,
and no seas nor doors nor walls
could stop the collision of light and shadow.

You might ask why his poetry
does not tell us of dreams or leaves,
or the great volcanoes of his native country.
Come and look at the blood on the streets . . .
Thus you described them
and now I can say—you confessed it often—
that the pupils of your eyes have widened,
and that because of her, touched by her bullet-riddled light
you went out again towards the world with your song
covered with blood from the streets.

Years have passed,
wars, the cruelest and saddest, have passed,
darkness and tears (how seldom the sun) have followed,
night has been in command for such a long time with its sword of
    shadow,
while you, Pablo, deep brother of peace,
of good for all men,
of the word flowing without chains
over mountains and seas,
Pablo of the solemn rivers and the most delicate petals,

of the starry skies without limits,
when you were more than ever the voice of hope,
when you raised the light to the peaks for your people,
(I heard it in the early morning hours), you were dying
full of pain, surrounded by assassins,
while blood ran in the streets of Chile.

Come now and look at his pillaged home,
his doors and windows smashed,
come and look at his books, already ashes,
look at his collection reduced to dust,
come and look at his body fallen
among the dregs of his broken dreams,
while blood still runs in the streets.

*Translated from the Spanish by Hermán Bleiberg and
Nancy Willard*

DAVID RAY

The Andes

for Neruda

Neruda
they dig to the Andes' spine
with augers as crooked as Nixon's shoes—
like a silkworm it spins
so smooth it is
and out of the mountain they make
their kimono—
the brocade on Madame Nixon's dragon
flakes on the floor, nitrates,
cobalt, diamond dust, oil
that rolls in tiny droplets
like an insect's tears.
And they whittle at your spine

13

knowing there's something there
something valuable, maybe gold
maybe radioactive
something they can use
words locked in the bone.

JEAN BRIERRE

Me Duele Chile*

> *To Isabel Allende*
>
> *("May my poem help keep alive that long-ago murdered spring,"*
> *—Pablo Neruda)*
>
> *an extract*

. . . Pablo
Pablo
Pablito,
You whose name sounds so much like *pueblo* and *pueblito*,
nothing is the same with you gone.
Sembene Ouamane's pipe was blown out by the cyclone,
an ember lies in the ashes of his gaze,
and his great Black laugh has grown older by a dawn.
Abdou Anta Ka's punctured tom-tom
has begun to beat wildly
like a sick man's heart running wild in its prison of flesh.
The voice of the muezzin of dawn,
collapses under the weight of splinters.
It is like the dry bed of a rush of sobs
that bristles with the debris of old wounds.
Klein's stained-glass Alexandrine breaks into crystal shards,
Ismet of Cairo, Nefertiti in profile,
the Pyramids liquid in the shrinking eye of the sun;
the gold thread of silence between sad lips,
forget the war to better endure death.
Anabelle feels that I am not well and calls me,

*I grieve for Chile   14

my delight in her smile drains away suddenly,
in the untranslatable osmosis of our souls.
—My far-off Anabelle, O my promised land,
wild island among the civilized noises
of the Champs Elysées,
they have murdered the epic soul of the Andes,
ransacked his retreat
on the mauve hill at sunset,
made an auto-da-fé
of "a new stage of his silence."
Anabelle, I feel ill . . .
And you whose name rhymes with dahlia,
maybe I would suffer less
if you had not gone away.
But your going and his death
were written in the lines of my palm . . .
The Araucan rebel receives the Nobel Prize,
the Araucan who refused the gilded exile of the embassy,
preferring his ceramics to crystal flutes,
his red-and-black poncho to a tuxedo.
Your death gives my solitude the dimensions of a Sahara.
The ghosts of suicides come to haunt me.
The edges of wounds I thought forever healed
begin to bleed and get feverish.
You are not dead, crucified like Christ,
but, like Spartacus, with the spittle of anger in your shout . . .
I waited for you so long in the "armpit" of La Boca
at Buenos Aires,
We were to visit the House of Slaves
at Goree this autumn
with Miguel Hernández and Asturias.
A flood of male talk,
a nocturnal beating of the tom-tom,
keep me from sleep.
I will stand watch at your grave the rest of my life.
But tonight, to keep from being overcome by vertigo
eluding the vigilance of the Kremlin guards,
I am going to stand watch
over the tomb of Lenin.

Translated from the French by Nan Braymer

LEO ROMERO

For Pablo Neruda

1

The sea has gone naked for you
she waits for you
her body gone quiet now

The rain has gone naked for you
falling perpetually towards you
in the heart of rain there is sobbing

The dew has gone naked for you
in the meadows of morning
in the unblossoming flowers of your dreams

2

I imagine one black tear
cried at night
and you in a room

Doors, ceiling and floor
flying away from you
like birds

3

It is not dew in the hair of the women
but tears; they have been crying in their hair
Crying every night knowing no other way to confront
the emptiness of your leaving

From the distant mountains pours a darkness
that washes over the desert
Washes over the spine-covered heart of the desert
with a water more bitter than tears

4

My dreams are of black moths
circling white, dying suns
And of black suns over white deserts
where scorpions blindly eat each other

My dreams are of black moths
circling white, dying suns

5

Your face bloomed briefly
like the cactus flowers

6

Must it be farewell, Pablo
I thought your singing voice would never die

The melodious bird
lies beneath the garden tree, its heart broken

EMILY PAINE

For the Spirit of Neruda

dedicated to the spirit of the three Pablos

Pablos of the sea and of the mountains
stringing the valleys with webs of eagles' nests
washing the cliffsides with winds of cyclones,
these continents of jungle and desert;
plains and rivers;
streams descending from a space in the sky
to traverse bare acres
where your plateaus straddle
the big top of this planet.

We of the still barren desert mourn your ascension.
We of the infant clover stand up to be larger than our tears.
We of the antelope forage our valleys in your name.

VOLKER BRAUN

Last Residence On Earth

For Pablo Neruda
(written on September 22, 1973)

Spilling from tanks in darkness
Octopuses suck on his Arcadian fence.
The private-eye roaches
Of the public regime squat
Sweating in their stupidity
On his stairway.
The eavesdropping ears
Of the militia hang
Like festering snot
On the telephone wires.
Immortal in their shame and Hispanic terror
Corpses wait, with cocked pistols,
Under his trees.
But this is certain:
In his besieged room the poet
Speaks as he has never before
In his incinerating life
The fatal truth.

Translated from the German by Hannelore Hahn

RAFAEL MENDOZA

This Pablo

It so happened that this Pablo was tired of being a man,
so he decided to set free for another place
with his way.
He was a resident of this poor earth
and for this he used to sing to the poor.
Without being a soldier he was always a captain
of the people
with his voice in the Andes, in the mines
and wherever he happened to meet burdened shoulders
underneath the sun each day.
Each day his heart sank with agony
from knowing that there were one hundred million
men working the earth for the insatiable oppressors.
At night he would reveal his enormous light
so the steps of the obscure travelers would be lit
in the horrible hour of the conspiracies
of gold, of shrewd vultures, of ambitions and guns.

He had an island of gentle sea-breezes
very near the ocean, with sirens and angels,
where the conch shells taught every mystery
of the sky, of water and of the fertilized earth.
There, above the sands, before the dark shoals of fish
he collected the events of the centuries.
He met at many times, the dawn
which would take refuge inside the moon.

His moonstruck life, his moonstruck days
waiting for the moment
when America would cover with one cloak
all her brothers in blood, speech, and misery.
Poor boy of dreams! Poor boy of anguish!

He was a resident of the earth.
And, it so happened that one day he was tired of being a man
so he decided to set free for another place
with his way.

Translated from the Spanish by Charles Hayes

MURIEL RUKEYSER

Neruda, The Wine

We are the seas through whom the great fish passed
And passes. He died in a moment of general dying.
Something was reborn. What was it, Pablo?
Something is being reborn: poems, death, ourselves,
The link dead in our peoples, the dead link in our dead regimes,
The last of our encounters transformed from the first
Long ago in Xavier's house, where you lay sick,
Speaking of poems, the sheet pushed away
Growth of beard pressing up, fierce grass, as you spoke.
And that last moment in the hall of students,
Speaking at last of Spain, that core of all our lives,
The long defeat that brings us what we know.
Meaning, poems, lifelong in loss and preference, passing forever.
I spilled the wine at the table
And you, Pablo, dipped your fingers in it and marked my forehead.
Words, blood, rivers, cities, days. I go, a woman marked by you—
The poems of the wine.

II. Light That Arrives

MATILDE URRUTIA NERUDA

Pablo's Death

One could say that Pablo was a happy man. This could be perceived in everything he wrote, even when he was forced to keep to his bed.

He had somewhat recovered from his illness, but the day of the *coup d'état* was a very trying one for him. When we learned of Salvador Allende's death, the doctor called me immediately and said: "Keep all the news from Pablo, for it could put him beyond recovery."

Pablo had a TV set in front of his bed. He would send his chauffeur to fetch all the newspapers. He also had a radio that got all the news. We heard of Allende's death through a Mendoza (Argentina) station, and this announcement killed him. Yes, it killed him.

On the day following Allende's death, Pablo awoke in a fever, with no access to medical care, because the head doctor had been arrested and his assistant did not dare to go as far as Isla Negra. Thus we were isolated without medical help. The days were passing and Pablo's condition was growing worse. At the end of the fifth day, I called the physician and told him, "We must take him to a clinic. He is most seriously ill."

All day he was riveted to the radio listening to stations in Venezuela, Argentina, and the Soviet Union. Finally, he grasped the situation.

His mind was perfectly lucid—absolutely clear till he fell asleep.

At the end of five days, I called a private ambulance to take him to a Santiago clinic. The vehicle was thoroughly searched during the trip, which disturbed him greatly. There were other brutalities, and that also affected him visibly. I was at his side. They made me get out, and searched me and the ambulance. It was terrible for him. I kept telling them: "It's Pablo Neruda. He is very ill. Let us through." It was frightful, and he reached the clinic in a critical condition.

Pablo died at 10:30 P.M., and no one was able to go to the clinic because of the curfew. I then had him transported to his Santiago home, which had been destroyed—books, everything. There we kept watch, and many people came, in spite of the times we were passing through in Santiago.

When we arrived at the cemetery, people came from everywhere, workers, all workers with hard, serious faces. Half of them kept shouting, "Pablo Neruda," and the other half replied: "Present." This crowd entered the cemetery singing the Internationale in spite of the repression.

Translated by Abraham Zitron

JOSÉ H. LLUBIEN

Neruda: Light That Arrives

For Emiliana Lopez Duprey

Where are you?
Where do you leave the light of your words?
Gone out!   Gone out!   Gone out!
What's your name now?
Where do you command heart-shaking words now?
Where do you keep yourself?
 Between ashes and white feathers
 Between the wings of the south wind
Flying, you're with young mules and ivory canes
With kettles and frying pans with Indian copper boilers
And stone chests
There / with boxes of teeth and gold molars

Nocturnal, sunken in time and water
By a watch of dead seconds and minutes
By a vigilance of bodiless hands and feet
Toward mountains and peaks
There / in the summits and topmost crests of diamonds of water
You keep yourself

II

Stage: Between streets and alleys of silk
Blood rises and falls, and rivers
With shocks and blows the tiger levels a village
And knocks down to the best bidder
Those accursed ones, those in the middle
The stool pigeons
Hangmen who trade night
            for gunpowder and death
Its Armageddon will come to that pestilence
Its end and justice
Is sure
The light that is on its way.

III

From the hills of Tarapaca
To the plains of Tierra del Fuego
He who watches from the heights and from volcanos
Is like a soul in pain
Haunter of Alameda
Of squares and Chilean lanes
Great wanderer of night and morning
He cannot rest
Uneasy like a torment of fire
He lunges forward declaring his presence
In a torrent of thunder and lightning!

Translated from the Spanish by Millen Brand

RUTH LISA SCHECHTER

Are We Saying All Your Verses?

For Pablo Neruda (1904–1973)

are we saying all your verses
            the green ones?
shaped like bread
shaped like houses going up
shaped ring on ring
shaped like Central America
pumping our heart's great vessel to Paloma
into peninsulas of feeling
aroused to being stanzas
tied to you in Guatemala
tied to you in Chile's glassy windows
bloodsmeared to the extremes
of our bodies
that tangible integrity
on the end of a line
vulnerable as fish on the angler's hook
trapped in the ocean that knows this

your poems born and reborn
are new light, new fire translating
the topaz stone of the Paraguays
cutting our lips all week

thinking of your heart's collapse
thinking of you in Santa María Clinic
thinking of loss going haywire
crying on the telephone
giving the message
we want everyone to come alive
shouting your goodbye
to bloody streets of Santiago where sadists
act out counterfeit theater
still killing the children of María and Pedro

you wanted to protect from signatures of pain
in view of executioners who have no eyes
in view of the world shuffling past
those thousands dead again
in the open square

are we saying all your verses
            the green ones?

JACK CURTIS

The House

In Pablo's house of stone and rain,
South between whale and night,
Higher on the ridgeback
We built together, sweat with the mortar,
Striking at the keel stones to see them sound,
Sending them into the walls like sisters and brothers,
Lofting the mighty timber trusses,
The artful rooftree,
The final banner.

When they came to Pablo's house,
We gave them Bread, Books, Water and Wine,
We opened all the secret closets,
We opened all the banks,
We opened all the gardens,
Air and light, laughter, guitars,
Macchu Picchu in its sombre agony, all of it,
We gave them all we had
And all we could salvage
And all our expectations.

In Pablo's house dark as a deep well,
The grey stones knew no tears,
We had embraced each one as a brother and sister

And mentioned we were leaving,
And sometimes would return at dusk
Or in a spring shower, or in times of fire
And exhaustion.
The stone ship surged on the ridgebone,
The bells rang Begin Again, Begin Again.

THOMAS McGRATH

A Warrant for Pablo Neruda

With the fury of cinders, with the despair of dusty
Great meat-eating birds stuffed under glass, with
The public stealth of rust on wedding rings,
The shriveled bureaucrats with flag-false eyes—
Smug as one-legged guides of the blind

Or politicians impersonating men—
Water their withered bible, loosen the night's black
Knife and now on the polo fields of the rich
Exercise the clanking hounds of illusion
And oil up a warrant for the twentieth century.

They are hunting for you, Neruda. And who now
Will stop them from stuffing the wild birds of the forest
With the blue fission of national neuroses? Who
Will found the myth of Copper? Who at Magellan's
Delta remember the ritual of forgiveness?

No one but you. No one but you. It is just.
They must hunt you, because of what they have forgotten:
The name of the buried miner. (The bronze face of wheat,
The river of indulgence that flowed from O'Higgins' side,
Dries in their heads like moss in a filing cabinet.)

And what of Bolívar's tears, curling like purple chips
From the lathes of usury? They go with you to the high

Andes where police cannot marshal a true man to hunt you—
No, though the Supreme Court, unhappily sane
And naked, run through the downtown streets, shouting

That laws have become just, black white, odd even—
No. The Conspiracy of October Lilacs is against them;
The Fronde of Innocence cocks a summer rifle,
The Union of Barley is on strike, and everywhere
An alchemy of resistance transmutes your flowering name.

JOSEPH BRUCHAC

Pine Cone

For Neruda/For Chile

*Pablo Neruda tells, in "Childhood and Poetry," the story of
a toy sheep and a pine cone. When he was a small child, the
toy sheep was thrust through a hole in the fence behind his
house, a gift from a child he never saw. Neruda placed a pine
cone which he adored, "Open, full of odor and resin . . ." in its
place.*

*"To feel the affection," he said, "that comes from those whom
we do not know . . . widens out the boundaries of our being,
and unites all living things. That exchange brought home to me
for the first time a precious idea: that all of humanity is some-
how together."*

The General sits with folded arms,
his jaw a bayonet aimed at the heart.
Dark glasses stare ahead
at history—a soccer stadium
filled with the rattling
applause of rifles.

I hold a pine cone
between my palms,

dried resin coats
its wooden leaves.
It fills my hands
with the smell of forests.
Small things are caught
in its recesses, a bit of blue lichen,
a strand from a spider's web, a single
seed, a feather, a dried leaf.

Imperfect as a human body,
burst open to give life to the cycle,
its wooden leaves seem fragile,
yet fibers within them hold.
It does not break,
even if stepped on
by a heavy boot.

The center of the cone holds darkness
as a burnt-out redwood can hold
the memory of a grove.
It knows its past,
even after the fall.

My hands and my poems
are covered with
the dirt of the pine cone,
a gift through a wall,
words which break down
all walls.

YUSUF AL-KHAL

For Neruda Upon His Death

There was once a man in the land
His land, our land everywhere
He was big, oxen-big, and a Word
Not the Word that was in the beginning
But the Word that is in the end.

He gave his Name to the Millions and Millions
They were poor and they were in sorrow
But they were the Millions, they were
The seed, the seaside seed, of Abraham
And the seal of the Spirit was upon them.

I loved you, Pablo Neruda, for a brother
Not a communist, nor a poetical brother
Nor the one who was in the Garden of Eden
Or the first fruit of an ancient overlord
I loved you just because you have lived and died:

For your life and death shall not be forgotten
You washed the feet of the Many
You climbed the hill of no return
You nailed your death on a lonely tree
Whose roots sprang up to Heaven.

Let me know where you are, Pablo Neruda
To go now and kiss your hand
If you are in the earth I will take a shovel
or a tear if You were in Heaven
Let me know for my sake and all.

Pablo Neruda

an extract

4—

You are flying alone, lonely.
Like Blake, Rimbaud and Whitman
you are obsessed with a love of liberty
and a hatred of the violence that works to destroy it.
Your odes, songs, shouts, blasphemies
weighted with human truth
penetrate to the palace and the barbershop
to mansion and to shanty
and they sing of man
in his three dimensions.
Of the man alone . . . bewildered
and lost in the uproar and turmoil
of the sick, grasping city.
Of the poor man . . . forlorn seaweed
lost on an immense ocean
of tremendous cosmic machinery.
You go alone. You leave behind long roads
seeds and vistas of virgin forests
open windows, transoms of light
through which one glimpses illimitable distances
and through which eddy and flow
the clamor of crowds, flavors of eternities.

5—

You are flying alone, lonely
among rubbish and spurts of fire,
among pursuing condors
among throatcutting and harping quetzals
among millions of bleeding wounded
between streets of the famished towns
that go to sup water from the table of God.

Pablo, you were the beginning and the culmination
of an enormous emotion
and the lyric, vibrant awareness
of our Indo-Hispanic America.
Neruda, you were the herald and profound announcer
of history . . . the link intrahistory
to our time and generation.
Visionary, prophet
obstinate oak tree of the Andes and the Amazons . . .

Translated from the Spanish by Ramona Weeks

ROBERT ROSENBERG

To the Memory of Pablo Neruda

You can be happy that the dogwood tree still blossoms
that the diamond-back terrapin does not cry out when eaten
that the needles of the yew berry do not bleed on your bones
and that sorcerers have turned the dawn into a prayer for reptiles.

What you do not realize, and will be saddened to hear,
is that the phallic sequoia has fallen from my teeth
and killed the snows of hidden hare and majestic elk.
That a canoe has capsized in the rapids of my swirling memory.
That a macaw has raped a marmoset with his watercolor breast
and the rings of the zebra have faded into the grass.

Magicians crawl thru the maze of my face
and steep cannibals in the cauldron of my heart.
Legends have drowned in the lakes of spiders
whose webs are garland with moist flames.

But you can be happy that the lioness bears spring
or saddened that entrails of words hang unnoticed from the giant
    eyelid of the sky.

ALLEN GINSBERG

To a Dead Poet

Some breath breathes out Adonais and Atlantis
Some breath breathes out Bombs and dog barks
Some breath breathes out silent over green snow mountain
Some breath breathes not at all

Now your shoes have no feet
Your socks have no ankles
    and toes to fill them
Your pants have no legs,
    your shirt no breast, no
    heart beating beneath
    your underwear,
your tie is a hole with no neck,
    your tie hanging over
your face no expression,
    your big nose no
    breath
your conch shell collection
    is empty, your skull
no brains to warm it and hear
    the echo of Canto General,
your poetry long as Chile your
    epics, verses, sonnets,
    line by line lie empty
your Revolution new Marxist
    People's Government
like poetry floating out of your mouth
like breath out of the mouth of
    one corpulent man,
empty as Death, year 1973,
    empty as South America
empty as Andes, empty as Life
    empty as Pablo Neruda.

    25 Sept.

34

ROBERT ZALLER

Lament For Neftalí Reyes

an extract

He would not want us to remember him
more than the schoolchildren slain
the professors who vanish
the anonymous blood on the floor
not more than the workers
stacked like wood in the cellar
nor the man who committed suicide
dozens of times
with the dozens of holes in his body
He would want to be remembered
as one who died with the rest
He is part of the earth now, the wave
part of the sorrow that mourns him
The poet is dead. We are his body.

HUGO STANCHI

A trilogy in memory of Pablo Neruda

an extract

ODE TO HORUS

He took his suit hanging from the cross
that was Chile that 11th of September
and he gave it to me and with imperious
voice said, "Put it on, because it is
now yours."

I looked at him as if he were an
apparition, the smoke out of a fire

35

or a myth and said, "They have
killed you, Pablo, it's all over."

He smiled and laughed and with the
crystal voice of an Andean spring
said, "Anarkos, friend of mine,
lover of the essence that is pure freedom,
do you really believe that we are dead?"
and with his left hand he
conjured a vision of breadmakers
rising the yeast that is the Spirit
of the People.

He repeated the offer; I protested in vain.
"The sleeves are too big, the waist is too
ample, the pants," but he did not hear me
replying, "We will fill you up with
adjectives, we will make you muscular
with verbs, you will be articular
compound-complex," and he helped me dress
and then poured gasoline over all
the clothes and lit a match.

Then he sought me out in the ashes and found
two calcinated tibias, three knuckles, a little
piece of pencil, a carbonized heart, a skull
with a yellow flower and a smile, and very
carefully he picked everything up—
bones, piece of pencil, flower, heart,
smile and skull and he tossed me to the
Chilean air where I became a peregrine falcon
that in being lashed by the wind, like the waves
lash the sands and the rocks
around Black Island, heard the sten-
torious voice of The Teacher saying,
"Do not cry, silly! Do not whisper
'E'li, E'li lama sa bachthani!'
HE is already with you! Sing rather sing
poet sing! Sing free! Sing love!

Sing light! Sing Peace! Sing world!"
and I, alone,
in that strange and lonely night, began
my solitary flight letting loose with
my talons the red seeds of the poetry
of Rebirth.

POET'S SONG

The Revolution saw me filthy, sick, hungry, with
rotten teeth and tumors and junky pains—i.e.
trading punches with a disinterested government
and a life that strangled and she stopped me
and with her bony hand she offered me a daisy
and said "Come with me. Through me speaks the
God that you are seeking."

I accepted the flower, i.e., I accepted the
first beautiful thing that I have received in
a long time and thought "Why not?"

Today I am part of the world. I exist where there
is hunger, injustice, poverty. I have neither
shirt nor shoes, but I walk free without shame
and my song is spear, my poems are arrows
and when I look at you in the eyes I
offer you a universe. Would you like
to come with me?
—

I will introduce myself: I am called "Nobody"
and those who exploit humanity when they call
me "commodity" insult human vision.

ED OCHESTER

For Neruda

an extract

i

The generals as always
are burning your books;
they were trained
at West Point and simply
cannot help themselves

IT&T and Anaconda
are paying assassins
a few of your poems . . .

ii

After your death our magazines review
only Russian writers in exile
if they are Christians
and advocate the return of the Czar.
We admire their form.

iii

The poets of North America
are ghosts visiting
burial mounds in Wisconsin
and Minnesota; they are in love
with the dead. If they could
they would slip under the chemical
prairies. They would walk
the lonely highways in Iowa
at night with fire in their hands.
They would immolate themselves
on a psychiatrist's couch in Dubuque
and make no noise.

Pablo was my better father,
teaching what patience I have with a knife
and the way of planting root vegetables and corn,
not to curse the soil;
teaching a man to get out of his coach—
Look! there are people in the forests, faces
in the prisons and the coal mines . . .

iv

These words are for Neruda.
Perhaps he will die.
Perhaps the generals will die
again with stakes through their hearts.
Perhaps the bankers and his poems
will turn back to the soil
like straw sandals rotting for a season.

Perhaps one day we will all visit together
the little museum in Wisconsin
where the loveliest thing he saw
was an embroidered heart.
Perhaps people will sing
even in the small republics,
cornfields nourished by blood.

DUANE LOCKE

Kaivalya

When I meditate, I visualize myself
surrounded not by Buddhas or Bodhisattas
but by countless Pablo Nerudas.
Each one wears a cap, very much
like the one worn by Hugh Fox,
and each Pablo Neruda stands on the ocean.
From each Pablo Neruda emanates white light
that changes into white water birds.

These birds splash the air
and from their feet fall blue drops
all over my floor that turns to sand and salt.
Each salt grain and each sand grain
has the voice of Pablo Neruda,
and directs me to follow the blue light
that emanates from my heart.
I follow the blue light and find a fern.
I put my ear to the stem and hear
Pablo Neruda, the moon, the sun,
earth, air, fire and water
all fused into one
and moving through the stem
to send out a new frond
that will unfold into a new existence.

IDA GRAMCKO

To Neruda Incommunicado

When men know
that a poet is not just one man more
but someone chosen by the deep subterranean strata
to raise up skies, symbols, citadels, signs,
when men know
that a lily isn't born as a sudden pureness
but is born crudely so that a handful of cotton
can be reworked by the poet into something rare, even
esoteric, mystical, magical, or human,
when men know
that true poets love freedom, then they can love fearlessly—
I'm not even afraid of my fantasies!—
and especially they can love the unpretentious, and be unpretentious,
since poetry isn't an intellectual hierarchy
but a strong, productive maternal impulse,
an eternal compulsion to groan and give birth,
something like a large-waisted life sowing without rest,

like one possessed to give birth,
to give light again
to a world, a sea, a bird, a plant,
a way of being an insecure womb
that constantly quickens with promise, protest, or supplication;
when it's felt—
I didn't know so much was lacking—
they will know that snow, that snow and cloud exist through talent,
that there's only snow when a poet has seen it,
that there's only cloud when a poet describes how white it is.
When that is felt
there will be a sad recollection of that remote time
when man—was it man?—submitted to being just an animal
and had no thought of being a heart, a dream, a soul.
Then, all will be clean and light.
Is so much missing for this future, this "then"
in which the policeman's boot will be known for what it is, a dirty
    diploma?
It will be the first day on earth.
And men who, like you, felt
cataracts of nails in their blood
because mindblown children lay down with their wounds in dung,
a silt of needles in their eyes,
for it hurts to see the sun if there's no one to see it in peace and
    abundance,
men like you will be loved.
Yes. It will be known some day.
You are one who has shared bread, sipped wine
with dusty fishermen and pale sheepherders.
You are one who never believed that
wheat and bunches of grapes were
the privilege of a few
but of all and especially those
who drew a fervor, a hymn, a breath from hunger.
Only then will it be known that a poem
is a shout of joy, a euphoric scream, a melodious song of anguish,
and right now I tell you
that about these brief sentences they'll say: it isn't a poem.
What does it matter? A poem is a child growing among rocks,

rivers, and oaks.
A poem is as secret
as a smiling, sobbing child being born.
It's quite a while now
from a very intimate womb
that I knew a
poem often grew
between tatters of hand and cheek,
between poverty-stricken eyelids that lie at one's feet, like remnants.
Nobody gives us any protection.
We bring our own protection
and we'll go on managing it, and among those who have no grace
as men,
but waste away as hermits.
In front of a fort not of marble but of wheat
and mild grapes,
the gray sentinels take their positions,
with no self-longing,
those whose clothes carry big
patches of dust,
then we're only a dust with odd trustfulness,
those who offer their foreheads so that the heroic hidden world
engraves its signs on them as if on rough blackboards,
sentinels watching for the kingdom,
and not only grayish but beginning to speak, prevailing
until the great alleluia breaks out among wasps, bitten lips,
trembling, loud under the horsefly.
Still believing that man
will one day know that the poet is more a vowel, or that
a concept,
because it is the flute of fever
that rises to others from phlegm and frost,
is a lute without aesthetic logic,
a very old harp whose strings
were born from open veins, from rustling bones,
and also from light that was ascending,
giving value to the bony cordage braided with arteries spilling out
watery blood.

Translated from the Spanish by Millen Brand

III.   Blues for Salvador

PRESIDENT SALVADOR ALLENDE'S FAREWELL SPEECH

over Radio Magallenes, September 11, 1973

Surely this will be the last opportunity I will have to address myself to you. The air force has bombed the towers of Radio Portales and Radio Corporacion. My words do not come out of bitterness, but rather deception, that they may be the moral punishment for those who betrayed the oath they took as soldiers of Chile, titular commanders in chief . . . Admiral Merino, who has self-designated himself commander of the armada . . . Mr. Mendoza, the callous general who only yesterday declared his loyalty to the government, has been named director-general of the carabineros [Chilean National Police].

In the face of these facts, the only thing left for me to say to the workers: I will not resign! Placed in a historical transition, I will pay with my life for the loyalty of the People. I say to you that I have the assurance that the seed that we plant in the dignified consciousnesses of thousands and thousands of Chileans cannot be forever crushed.

They have the power, they can smash us, but the social processes are not detained, neither with crimes, nor with power. History is ours, and the People will make it.

Workers of my country: I want to thank you for the loyalty which you always have shown, the trust which you placed in a man who was only the interpreter of the great desires of justice, who gave his word that he would respect the Constitution and the law, and that I did.

In this definitive moment, the last thing which I can say to you is that I hope you will learn this lesson: foreign capital, imperialism united with reaction, created the climate for the armed forces to break with their tradition, that of General Schneider, and which Commander Araya reaffirmed, a victim of the same social sector which today finds them in their houses, waiting to retake power, by strange hands, to continue defending their huge estates and privileges.

I address myself above all to the modest woman of our land, to the peasant woman who believed in us, to the working woman who worked more, to the mother who knew of our concern for her children. I address myself to the professionals, to those who were working against the auspicious sedition carried out by the professional schools, schools of class which also defend the advantages which capitalist society gives them.

I address myself to the youth, to those who sang, who gave their joy and spirit to the struggle. I address myself to the Chilean man: to the worker, the peasant, the intellectual, to those who will be persecuted because fascism has already been present in our country for many hours: those terrorist actions which blew up bridges, cutting railway lines, destroying oil and gas pipelines, in the face of the silence of those who had the obligation of pronouncing themselves. History will judge them.

Probably Radio Magallenes will be silenced, and the calm metal of my voice will not reach you: it does not matter. You will continue to hear me, I will always be beside you or at least my memory will be that of dignified man, that of a man who was loyal.

Workers of my country: I have faith in Chile and in her destiny. Other men will overcome this grey and bitter moment where treason tries to impose itself. May you continue to know that much sooner than later the great avenues through which free men will pass to build a better society will open.

Long live Chile! Long live the People! Long live the Workers!; these are my last words. I am sure that my sacrifice will not be in vain; I am sure that it will at least be a moral lesson which will punish felony, cowardice and treason.

Translated from the Spanish by the Common Front For Latin America (COFFLA)

KARL VENNBERG

First Day of Autumn 1973

To the memory of Salvador Allende

an extract

. . . Who among us can fail to hear
the silence in the wind?

Over there the dogs lick the tongues of the dead,
over there the birds lift the dead to heaven in their bills.
The story rolls up out of the ocean,
and it is like a dog with shark's jaws which yelps and sniffs.

Here we live under the cloud.
Here we live in a thinning light.
Here we live—while over there freedom is nailed to a tree to die.

Who gives us the words which save us,
the patient words for the long road?
Who lights our night while our sorrow buries its face in its hands?
Who fills us with a spring light
where the bees can fly out into the sun,
where the night is warm with birdsong
and we all again can sleep in the open?

All we hear is the night wind
which whirls round with the agony of the murdered.

Translated from the Swedish by Jonathan Brand

GEOFFREY RIPS

Resurrection: For Allende

> *"I rise every hundred years*
> *when the people wake up."*
> *—Neruda*

They're dancing the tango in Tierra del Fuego
at the end of the earth where the seas
pound the glaciers, where souls rise
like steam from the ice under sunfire. Naked for Christmas

they're whirling the robes of the bald missionary
pointing to the cross in their eyes,
to the stars in their teeth, to the riveted
crucifix nailed to the heavens.

A new star has appeared on the celestial axis,
burning blue with the fire of the ice of the ocean.
With that star in their foreheads and ungirded loins,
they're dancing the tango in Tierra del Fuego.

MICHAEL SZPORER

elegy for allende

an extract

. . . salvador allende is dead.
slumped over the sofa soaked with his lips
where the dead blossom like hot flowers.
the banners of flaming rosebushes
are barbed wire in santiago
santiago of jagged nights and of discolored days
who could see you and forget?

those who have strength but not reason
who measure their reasons by bank accounts
and feed on copper flesh and copper hearts
have speeches severed from their elbows
with shapeless bayonets. newspapers are cleansed.
pencilmarks mapping out the world are readjusted
poems are burned.

TANURE OJAIDE

Chicho

(For Salvador Allende Gossens)

THE EAST was his guardian
And factories his fortress;
His was a new and narrow road
Whose goal promises great harvest
But sudden light startles
Who live in darkness.

An age is lived baring itself
Before jungle laws
    innocence or dirt
    and innocence is death;
When mad Santiago dogs mated
With a menstruous mother,
They debauched beauty.

Travel slow and warily on a new road.

And the oracular truth came to pass
That the black Eagle of the Hemisphere
In its fanatic jealousy devours
Whoever models life beyond sunset horizon
And so La Moneda was perforated and smoked;

Thirteen bullets kill only a man.

The cold spread by the starry casualty
Has benumbed yearning for better alternatives
Has shocked seeking new directions
As the Eagle fondles epileptic dogs
But thirteen bullets kill only a man;
Suffice that the people wept and resist
Even after their comrade's earthed;

Allende is an idea; he's forever.

A. APPERCELLE

To Chile—To Allende—

The sun
the bloodying
sea
cameras
        snap—
The water is transparent
white between our fingers
    it flows
"El Fascismo-el Fascismo"
—Take your guitar
            Chilean
and play   play
until our arteries burst
don't let the dust
swallow your brain
Strike!
        the women
will give birth to grenades.

Translated from the French by Serge Gavronsky

D. H. MELHEM

Homage to Allende

I.

Allende
Chile wriggles
to swallow you
who have been made
to eat death
as a wafer of preparation

having been priest/physician
to the cut wind
that partially returns
a constant
just apportioning

you will be
the serpentine
remedy
and in its skin
the fire

II. LOS ROTOS

the act of flesh
breaking open its first wine
anointing death
broken into odes and howling
the bowels' terror   the bladder's honey
broken into their mercy and this memorial curse

rotos
the incense of your stacked bodies
invades the roots of roses
and makes you whole with the field of that
dispersing earth   its fragments
seeking each other
like truth

TOBIAS BERGGREN

Poem From Gotland, September 1973

To The Memory of Salvador Allende

1

Day of boredom, congenitally malformed verses, "start over"
Evening now, almost freezing, dark, wind from the north
Airport lighttower
                    half-heartedly blinking
    Rain tonight
Kid's dropping off to sleep, wants to know
    how come we can fly in our dreams?
Cold day, gone
    Tonight, they'll murder Allende
I have no idea
                Can't even fly west
Thoughts on the starving continents
    sit in the brain like freezer-trays
Blood, a clouding over
                  A red pattern, running
Outside, the northwind moves in the nettles, big animal

2

Out there people are looking for a place to sleep
For something to eat
                some kind of meaning
Can't say I'm happy, but I'll last the night
Nor is communism happy tonight
    but that will pass
Murders and such will pass
Murderers never understand this
They might as well take the next step:
                        shoot themselves

3

My angry ruminations reach no one
        on the other side of the planet
Lighttower winking, with some innuendo now?
I'm losing power
                        even over myself!
Split
        Split and Gold
Not to lose power over ourselves
        we have to dismantle political power
Not to dare leave all political power
        to the people
                        is to distrust oneself
Too bad
Because there is no other power we can rely on
Those who lack confidence in themselves
        split the body of socialism
Tonight the murderers
        are charging into those cracks again

4

Lighttower beam splits the darkness
                                over and over
        Dreams of flying are being dreamed
Tonight we're alone
                        Animals in a pupa's dream

5

Socialism is hurting
        where the narrow wing
of Chile
        grows from the Earth's back

Translated from the Swedish by Anselm Hollo

GAYL JONES

Más Allá

An old man with onions on his breath.
"This is a country where they kill you for dreaming.
One must go *más allá* to dream.
One must go *más allá. Allende*.
Beyond those trees, beyond that river,
beyond those mountains. *Allende*.
This is a country where they kill you for dreaming."
He has a basket.
It is black inside his basket.
He says it is full of onions and sardines.
I see nothing.
He says it is prophets' food.
Perhaps only prophets can see.
He tells me to reach in my hand.
("You see by feeling too.")
I am afraid to reach in my hand.
He asks if I am afraid of a kiss.
I say, "No."
He kisses the side of my mouth.
I reach in my hand.
It comes out smelling like fruit.
He has salt in his eyes.
He is squeezing a snail in his fist.
He tells me this is a place where they kill you for dreaming.
"Go on, now," he says. "Go on.
The air here is already corroding my shoulders.
Do you know what they are afraid of?
They are afraid our dreams might break into flesh."

GARY ESOLEN

Dialectic: To the Victims of History

(for Salvador Allende)
September, 1973

The last tomatoes
are gathering light
in the bedroom window.
Something will come of it.
The red slice of sun
over the Andes
will end in the ocean.
The gentle lady at the bank
is glad for the price of gold,
her stocks are rising,
money pleases her.
The bulldozers have made a place
for eleven miners in Carletonville
and the police have explained:
we had no choice,
they went berserk, demanding
more wages.
The hickory logs
smell like sausage
and our pig is ready to kill
and doesn't know it.
Even that ignorant tremor
shakes at my spine
and the pulp of tomato
leaks in my hand
like a law of nature.
Allende is dead.
The will make use of him,
if they can,
like last night's dinner
of meat pie and wine;
and Kennecott copper

is up three points,
and the sun turns up again
over the Andes
like a bad penny
and the ocean will rise up against it
and I can feel the mountains
turning away.

ANTAR SUDAN KATARA MBERI

Blues for Salvador

THERE ARE
NIGHTS when emotions twist
white tornadoes suck up sanity's roots

THERE ARE
DAYS when senses cyclone
blue hurricanes rip and run
slay cities of the blood

THERE ARE
WEEKS when our lot of suffering
is endlessly a whip flogging my brain's back
our flesh running raw

THERE ARE
MONTHS when teeth turn to grindstones
gnash themselves to nubs

pulverizing
load stones of pain
leave vacuums
where only sores and silver can abide
or hide

THERE ARE
YEARS when we suck naked storms
YEARS when we suck raw sun's fire
YEARS when we suck mountains
                              buildings
                              cars
                              trains
                              planes
trying to lend order to our lives

THERE ARE
THESE DAYS, WEEKS, MONTHS, YES, EVEN YEARS
EVEN CENTURIES

when our nights are fugitive futures
dreams eluding us, leaving nothing
save rattles and a beggarman's cup

to ring empty in the hollow
space of copper nights and monopolies' face

or to die in the clean
honest fight.

LEE BAXANDALL

Neruda's Last Poem

The air of Chile is transparent,
but hermetic
        the coma of sinking,
        the coma of last thinking . . .
darkening.

I have heard it from the Army barracks,
        the generals think already on the words for my body,

Communism they hate—but Neruda?
"A national treasure."
What should I think?

Do I stand with the idea whose time has come, and
whose stature they despise?
Then, when my body is gone, does my name become dust?

Cancer makes my thoughts hurry.
But fame makes my bravery falter.

Had Che died insignificantly, of Cancer? Would his
impact linger?

The Army thinks well of me, the army is gathering
in its barracks,
Allende alone, silhouetted in his window—I am told.

Allende may soon go over the doorsill of the Moneda,
        with his government,
                to death.

A legend.

What shall I be? Shall the twenty songs of love and life
be followed by
                        nothing?

Allende rises from his chair, he walks
        down the staircase, towards the doorsill,

                rifles point at him, I hear bombs,—

Let me assure that the journey of Orpheus to the Netherworld
        does not prove companionless. . . .

        I shall step upon the shirttails of Salvador, the ride
will be endless.

IV. Tract for General Pinochet

Last week, I slipped through a side door into the Santiago city morgue, flashing my junta press pass with all the impatient authority of a high official. One hundred and fifty dead bodies were laid out on the ground floor, awaiting identification by family members. Upstairs, I passed through a swing door and there in a dimly lit corridor lay at least 50 more bodies, squeezed one against another, their heads propped up against the wall. They were all naked.

Most had been shot at close range under the chin. Some had been machine-gunned in the body. Their chests had been slit open and sewn together grotesquely in what presumably had been a *pro forma* autopsy. They were all young, and, judging from the roughness of their hands, all from the working class. A couple of them were girls, distinguishable among the massed bodies only by the curves of their breasts. Most of their heads had been crushed. I remained for perhaps two minutes at most, then left the building.

The next day I returned to the morgue with a Chilean friend so that I would have a witness. I also took along a camera. As I walked through the swing doors of the corridor, the sickly sweet smell of the decomposing bodies almost knocked me back. There were more bodies, perhaps 70, and they were different from the day before. Just as I was pulling the camera from my jacket, a man in a white coat walked through the doors at the other end of the corridor. "What do you want?" he asked. "I'm looking for the bathroom," I said. "Come with me," he said. As I followed him, I took a sharp right and ran out of the building. He shouted after me but did not try to follow. I did not have the courage to try again. Later, in my hotel room, my friend burst into tears. "These were my countrymen," he cried. "My God, what has happened to us?"

Most middle- and upper-class Chileans have no idea what is happening. Many do not believe the stories about slaughter in the *poblaciones*: many simply don't much care. "Why should we?" a Chilean lawyer asked me over an expensive lunch in a wealthy section of Santiago. "I don't believe the stories you tell me, but after the things the supporters of Salvador Allende have done to Chile, they deserve whatever happens to them."

ALAIN BOSQUET

Tract For General Pinochet

Every twenty years
The black orchid of hate
sprouts in my lungs
And if on this night, it is blooming
It is because of you, General Death

Every 10 years
The jeering nettle of fury
bursts one of my eyeballs
And if right now, I am stone blind
It is because of you, General Death

Every 5 years
The iris of scorn explodes in my guts
And if tonight my bowels
Are oozing out of me
It is thanks to you, General Death

Every spring the violet of suicide
Caresses my forehead
And if tonight,
my head has ten holes in it
It is your fault, General Death

Every Thursday,
the hemlock of revenge
offers me its glass of poison
And just tonight my throat longs to taste it
because of you, General Death

Every dawn
the rose awakens me
with her own special dawn, but
this morning she never got here
because you killed her, General Death

Translated from the French by Lillian Lowenfels

TOM WAYMAN

The Return

The poet comes back.
After the agony in the great stadiums
suddenly converted into prisons:
the torture of the young woman
in the corridors under the bleachers,
the rape and beating of the journalist's wife
while he is watching, the daily executions,
the electrode making contact again and again
on the body of the student strapped face-up on the table:
its black point darting in like the tongue of a snake
now spearing the scrotum with terrible pain, now the tip
of the penis, now the inside of the lower lip,
the nipples, the tongue, now the eye is forced open
and the electrode brought down toward the pupil . . .

After his body is stilled, the poet returns.
He knows that no one jailed the former Minister of Health
when the new government began for the first time
to distribute milk to the poor.
But the hands of a woman who worked in that program
now never stop shaking.
No one wished to interrogate the local executives
of a foreign mining company
about the long years of sorrow and sweat wrung out of Chile.
But there is a miner who lay on the concrete and bled inside
from the kicks of the police, until he died.

And no one sent for a squad of torturers from America
to investigate those Americans found living in Santiago
after the election. But a certain unit of the Brazilian military
instructed in the American school in Panama, and in their own
    country
flew in to begin processing their countrymen
discovered after the coup to have previously fled into Chile.

And there is a woman who heard so much screaming
she can no longer utter a sound.
There is a body dropped from an Air Force truck
into the street of a slum, that only on close examination
can be seen to have been a woman.

But the poet comes back.

His breath, his voice, his book
once again begins journeying.
His country goes down again
into the horrible night of its continent
but the poet continues to move.
Everywhere he comes to the poor like a man in trouble
and is taken in or not depending on their nature.
Those who receive him risk everything
just as though they hid again the living fugitive
but, as before, when he leaves he departs as their friend.
Those of the poor who are fearful, and turn him away
go on being poor, being frightened, still waiting
for the miraculous knock on the door that they know
will one day arrive to show them a better life.

The poet goes on. His words
are specks of light gleaming out of the darkness.
Death surrounds us all, but his words
go on speaking out of the blackness.
Hunger still sits in the stomach
like an egg soured into a chemical burning in the guts.
The muzzle of a gun is still pressed against the head of a man
who is shot before he can say a single syllable.
The voice of the poet is powerless to stop this.
The man who is beaten, his front teeth
snapped off under the sticks of the police
—he, too, loved the sound of the fresh salt wind
pouring in continuously over the waves of the sea beach . . .

But to everyone left numb
in the silence between these cries of agony and despair

the poet's voice goes on talking, calmly, persistently.
Also through the long drudgery of a lifetime
it keeps offering to those who have lost them
the words that mean a gift of the earth.

The poet says: "They burned my house in Madrid,
the house of flowers, geraniums, and a green horse.
They pulled down my house at Isla Negra,
brought down its great ceiling beams carved with the names
of dead companions, lowered my flag: a sea-blue, with a fish on it
held it and let free by two chains.
And when I saw the house of poetry was destroyed again
I knew that poetry now would be most needed elsewhere.

"So I began traveling. When I was alive
I took my place in the struggle. Now I am dead
my voice still speaks, ringing like a vast silence
which is really a mouth, filled up one by one
by those who take up my cry, which is their cry,
sounding our words together, drowning out torture
and the police, louder, drowning out hunger and fear,
speaking our life on this planet as loud as we can
until at last we drown out death."

GILBERT LANGEVIN

Anti-Cancer Concert

in homage to Pablo and Walter

The pentagonic west is oxidizing away
they're murdering liberty
Neruda, Chile, Allende
three funerary notes
in the concert of the universe

everywhere there's a clear view
of embryos of death and misery
the world has become a graveyard
of self-destruction

While Nixon and Kissinger
play poker
with the military
from edge to edge of the earth
caca—pipi—tatalism
distributes its toys, its rattles
and every country claims
its little pinochet

faites vos jeux faites vos jeux
the day is coming when it won't work
a cyclone of anger
will smash those who kill

Translated from the French by Nan Braymer

CHRISTINA MORRIS

Memo

From: El Farolito
To: General Augusto Pinochet Ugarte
Copies: Mitchell Sharp
            Andrew Ross
            Multinational Corporations
            International Capitalists.

Remember *this*:
"Blue dwarfs beget
Red giants become
White stars emit

Blazing pathfinders
Soaring
To a human Love-Sun.

Black holes
You dig for others
Will swallow *you*
With one small golpe.
You, fascist dwarf,
Smaller than nothing
For you are dying
Universally
Unloved."

Witnessed this day by
Cosmic eyes
Eternally agape.

ELENA WILKINSON

Chile: Elegía de la Venganza

i

Wrap the man well inside the soft arms of a child.
Shelter his face with black September roses.
We have no lights here. Nothing stays now.
There is such cold.

ii

Our seasons come to us so bloodlessly here.
Who remembers? Who possesses memory?
We stay inside our houses. We talk quietly in groups.
Where are our eyes, we ask, what of them?
Someone lights a fire. Someone begins to sing.
Someone hears us; dark fish move bloodlessly inside the sea.

They begin their solemn breathing.
They are far away. But they are waiting.

iii

Cover the body with the hearts of animals.
Let it be protected by their blood.
Our door makes noises. Wood begins to weep water.
Water seeps beneath the door. Smell of scales, whatever is waiting.
And cold: there is such cold.
Someone asks for a knife, holds it, raises an arm: it is
A small child, he cries *how have I come here?*
There is such cold. Who can remember?

iv

Everyone sits inside the house.
Everyone repeats prayers. Everyone sits quietly in groups.
Something waits outside the door. The child waits here.
He raises his arm, again and again.
The child is waiting; he remembers; he is ready.
It is cold.
The body is covered with blood.
Let it be protected by blood!

CAROL TINKER

"Another Defenestration in Prague"

for Fernando Alegría

At Mireya's beach house
we are friends, we are eating flan
we are discussing the 15,000 killed in Chile
we are talking about technology
we are discussing international control of finance
we are describing the United States

we stare hopefully at each other
        out of our own hopelessness
the blood is too recent
telephones:
                "How is Raphael?" "Raphael is very well"
                "How is Susanna?" "Susanna is sick"
                "How is Manuel?" "Manuel is very ill"
                "How is. . . . ."
I do not have the habits of power
I don't know how to use these telephones
The corpses are too new

NELSON ESTUPIÑAN BASS

A Candle for Pablo

Pablo
brother Pablo People,
where have they been, those frozen
leftover snakes who now are longing
to push time backward?
In what Pentecost
and in which Pentagon
or in which prayer-bench
did they administer their diabolic hosts
and drink their antihuman wine?

Pablo of all of us
Pablo of Always,
in what upside-down world
could these mistaken arsonists
turn off the sun and with their daggers
cut up the air
and close the road to apples,
camouflage bombs in embraces,
put poison into roses,
and thorns onto the sugar plants?

In which crushed grape,
in which malignant wineskin
did they collect the death they now distribute
in Chile, tulip of the sea?

Brother Pablo Forever,
upright in life and its reverse:
how we suffer to see Chile without words,
this Chile without writings or mail carriers,
its feet dragged from its path,
this Chile without voices in the streets
this Chile without songs by night,
Chile in which the hostage has no dreams!

Pablo,
Pablo of all the seas and stars,
Pablo of all the people of the world,
how it hurts to see your light so darkened,
to see you, Chile, exiled in your land,
to see the military winds
aiming to kill your mighty voice
the treacherous rape of your sunrise,
the trembling lives in embassies
the degradation of the seas and stadiums,
words burnt,
the doors' crossbars carefully closed,
the miserable cannibals' delight,
the mercenary curfew on the bridge,
and drinking one another's health
with all of all the evils made in USA!

Not illness, as they say, killed you,
no,
Neruda,
what killed you was the suffering of Chile,
hanging her head
her withering star by her side.

But,
how they forget,
brother Pablo Love
Pablo Hope
Pablo of all idioms and metres,
Pablo Tall,
the tallest of them all,
how they forget Hitler,
his carnival of blood and his parades
his unspeakable courts of skeletons,
and his sad pieces of discarded night.
When even children know that by tomorrow
after this prefabricated eclipse of the sun
the inexorable great fire will come
and precisely at the moment of the ashes
Chile will come back,
with its recovered civil light,
to the road of men,
Pablo Sun,
Pablo River,
Pablo Thunder and Lightning,
Pablo Chile
Pablo of the Revolution.

Translated from the Spanish by Lenore Veltfort

PIERO SANTI

For Chile—Love

Friend Juan of the blue glance
you flinched when
I told about you about your land
about the red cock who wouldn't yield
to the killer-worms
lodged in our guts;

Florentine olive trees around us
stiff pale contorted enemies
like the generals in Chile;
nature is always enraged
when
her sons are cut down by
black arms
never blue or red
but black
like the muck in city sewers.
That place over the Andes
will survive
where blood is sainted;
but here blood is inane
unspilled onto the olive trees;
our history stinks of stagnation
and you good Juan see
that only the future-charged young
understand how to shout
and sing for Chile;
in the silent Florentine night
the young rushed
toward San Lorenzo,
I took you by the arm
I saw faraway sorrow in your face.
Blood of the dead-alive
curdle, knot the throat
of the coward-plague in Santiago.
Here softness scars us
we race drunken over the rubberized-motorized-roads
prophecies are always miles away,
we don't see
how the Andean crags
can voluptuously marry our sweet mountains,
we don't see
ourselves gelded,
our blood hardly pink.
Blood of the dead-alive
curdle, knot the throat.

Harder men will spark
the golden lights of battle,
the nervous nights
in ambush-suspense
when life is flimsy and senseless.
Your earth will still be yours,
Juan, and some morning in a red dawn
you'll set out to redeem
Santiago, Valparaiso
the humane man who awaited death
to save even us
the Europeans hamstrung
and tongueless.

Translated from the Italian by Vinnie-Marie D'Ambrosio

HARVEY MUDD

The Near Sierra

an extract

It's Guernica again,
the stukas savaging democracy.
The planes driven
by vast
international
engines.

And my wife, who's Mexican,
wept when Chile fell,
and cried, "Each Indian woman
is the widow of Allende";
and cried, as if I had done it,
"Pero Zapata vive
with the angels,

in the sierra."
With his barefoot angels,
in the near sierra.

LOUISE GAREAU-DES-BOIS

Dream of the Other America

If you just keep your mouth shut
when so many are dying,
if you just listen
when it's time to speak out,
what's left but to build a great bonfire
for all of us, holding hands,
to jump in.

What a great blaze that would make—
cowards and ass lickers
and high-minded bastards
who walk around always
with placards lettered
SPECTATOR!

How can you just look on
when down there
murder is going on?
How can you keep your mouth shut
when just a few
own the earth?

Only people with dirty hands will get to heaven,
far, far away from the two Americas . . .

Translated from the French by Walter Lowenfels

74

PEDRO VERA

Chile, the wretched beasts . . .

Coastal Chile, my old friend
above your breakwaters
I unraveled my first storm
and love enveloped me with its rainbows.
I received the winds from your four borders
and entered your seas as if I were entering
    a woman.

Ah, impervious cordilleras with your frenzied snows—
Forestral Park with your celestial goats—
Mapacho full of tattered wanderers—
Oh, soaring of your wine cellars—
Oh, the bearded ocean that hugs you and
    is your praise

Today the gorillas, the wretched Yankee beasts
left their dens and came out to smudge the air
and now there is no snow, no sea, no grape,
    nothing.

They trampled the flower and polluted the seed
assassinated Allende, the purest Chilean.
They deface all that they touch with their cow dung.

Chileans, built of sea and sacrifice
the word I have to say to you is very small,
and this hand is so little that I must
press on your hand—
only blood now,
only the lasting blood to save your star!

Translated from the Spanish by Charles Hayes

V. The Chilean Singer

MIGUEL CABEZAS

Victor Jara Died Singing

*An eyewitness account**

On September 11th, in the Stadium, Victor went down to the arena and came near one of the doors from which new prisoners entered. Here he collided—in a bottleneck—with the commander of the prison camp. The commander looked at him, made a tiny gesture of someone playing the guitar. Victor gave an affirmative sign with his head, smiling sadly and candidly. The military man smiled to himself, as if congratulating himself for his discovery. He called four soldiers and ordered them to hold Victor there. Then he ordered a table to be brought and to be put into the middle of the arena so that everybody could see what took place immediately thereafter. They took Victor to the table and ordered him to put his hands on it. In the hands of the officer ("I have two beautiful children and a happy home," he declared days afterwards to the foreign press) rose, swiftly, an ax.

With one single stroke he severed the fingers of the left hand and, with another stroke, the fingers of Victor's right hand. The fingers fell to the wooden floor, trembling and still moving, while Victor's body fell heavily down.

A collective outcry from six thousand prisoners was heard. These twelve thousand eyes then watched the same officer throw himself over the fallen body of the singer and actor Victor Jara and begin to hit him while he cried:

"Now sing, you motherfucker, now sing," and kept on hitting him.

Nobody who was near can ever forget the face of the officer, ax in hand and with disheveled hair over his forehead. It was the face of bestiality and unbridled hatred.

*Jara, 27, was Chile's most popular folksinger. Cabezas was head of Chile's Quimantu publishing house.

Victor received the blows while his hands were dripping blood and his face was rapidly turning violet.

Unexpectedly, Victor laboriously raised himself to his feet and, with unseeing eyes, turned towards the bleachers of the Stadium.

His steps were faltering, knees trembling, his mutilated hands stretched forward like those of a sleepwalker.

When he came to where arena and bleachers meet, a deep silence ensued. And then his voice was heard crying:

"All right, comrades, let's do the señor commandante the favor!"

He steadied himself for a moment and then, lifting his bleeding hands, began to sing, with an eager voice, the anthem of the Unidad Popular, and everybody sang with him.

When those six thousand voices were singing Victor marked the time with his mutilated hands. On his face was a smile—open and released—and his eyes shone as if he were possessed.

This sight was too much for the military. A volley, and Victor's body began to fall forward as if he were bowing long and slowly in a reverence to his comrades. Then he fell down on his side and remained lying there.

More volleys followed from the mouths of the machine guns, but those were directed against the bleachers full of the people who had accompanied Victor's song.

A veritable avalanche of bodies came down, riddled with bullets, rolling to the arena. The cries of the wounded were horrible. But Victor Jara did not hear them anymore. He was dead.

Translated from the Spanish by Lenore Veltfort

JAMES SCULLY

Now Sing

NOW sing: the guards howling
beat him with obscenities.
    But he did.
His legend is
He was singing
                 Venceremos
when they shot him.
Even for them, it was too much

they killed him,
they couldn't kill him enough.

Victor Jara
        sin guitarra,
who'd held out with bloody stumps
                       and sung

EAMON GRENNAN

The Chilean Singer

(In Memory of Victor Jara)

No! white bird you're no
dove no sign you are
an albino pigeon shitting
on skyscrapers citizens monuments
you'll never sing to me
of lemonade & hard cider

They broke both his hands
bone after bone after bone
that once like swift swallows flitted

81

over ready strings to start
the children singing; those
swift strings stopped
the children are no longer singing
of lemonade & hard cider

They broke his teeth
trapped his tongue in blood
to throttle his singing
he went on singing
of lemonade & hard cider

They broke his spine:
in the hills a white bear
with a machinegun clubs
stone dead a single swallow
Oh father the woods are burning
the birds & the squirrel & the small deer
will die won't it hurt won't
we miss the singer's song
of lemonade & hard cider

They machinegunned him
full of bleeding mouths
tongues running dry   his voice
singing was clean as gravel
under shallow water, now
it gags on his own blood not
on lemonade or hard cider

Silence is last of all
silence in the streets the woods
silence in the air the hills
silence in the classroom turned morgue
silence the stranger in that heap of bodies
silence in the dead room as his wife enters
silence in the shout of a sleepwalking guard
silent white bears have wakened us to nightmares
of lemonade & hard cider
he becomes his wife's silence

LINDA LIZUT

Untitled

the taste of the land is sharp
chile picante
sugar cane does not grow
in the high desert

sting of native music
red ants fill the throats
of the conquerors

there is no honey
even for the children
who beg
for sweets

we give them
the fingers of Victor Jara
cut off
with a machete

the little ones suck
blood drooling
from the corners
of their mouths
they chew the pulp

raw music
refined
sugar washed in blood

delicate bones
picked clean
strum lullabies
late into the night

waves follow the moon
ancient gong
hammered gold mask
of death

JUNE JORDAN

Poem: To my sister, Ethel Ennis, Who Sang "The Star Spangled Banner" at the Second Inauguration of Richard Milhouse Nixon, January 20, 1973

In Memory Of Another Singer, Victor Jara

gave proof through the night
that our flag was still there

on this 47th inauguration of the killer king
my sister
what is this song
you have chosen to sing?

and the rockets red glare
the bombs bursting in air
my sister
what is your song to a flag?

to the twelve days of Christmas
bombing when the homicidal holiday shit tore forth
pouring from the B-52 bowels loose over Hanoi and the skin
and the agonized the blown limbs the blinded eyes the
silence of the children dead on the street and the
incinerated homes and Bach Mai Hospital blasted and
drowned by the military the American shit vomit
dropping down death and burying the lives the people
of the new burial ground
under the flag

for the second coronation of the killer king
what is this song
you have chosen to sing?

my sister
when will it come finally clear
in the rockets red glare
my sister

84

after the ceremonial guns salute the ceremonial rifles
saluting the ceremonial cannons that burst forth a choking
smoke to celebrate murder
will it be clear
in that red that bloody red glare
my sister
that glare of murder and atrocity/atrocities
of power
strangling every program
to protect and feed and educate and heal and house
the people
(talking about *us*/you and me talking
about *us*)

when will it be clear to you

which night will curse out the stars with the blood
of the flag
for you
for enough of us

by the rockets red glare
when will it be clear
that the flag that this flag is still there is still
here and will smother you smother your songs

can you see
my sister
is the night
and the red glaring blood clear at last
say

can you see
my sister

say you can see
my sister

and sing no more of war

BOB ARNOLD

Faraway, Like The Deer's Eye

Ah yes, now I believe I know
A cool breeze and very early morning
The wood thrush that breaks from the pasture
The fences have all been mended
Here and there, new barbed wire, animal hair

I think of Jara, Victor—
By Jesus as they sliced off your fingers
And you kept to the last moment
Something loving, say your sister, far in your belly
Then they beat you like the backside of a horse
And it all fell— my chore bucket spilled
Suddenly in Vermont

I may still have the gathering of birds
The pull of this long river
Where I wade to my waist and undo my hair and wash slowly
Strong sweat and black flies
A quiet day with the saw
Now near its end

But Chile stays— forever
How in the hell can you ask me to forget
A father dragged down from an attic
And pumped into a throbbing scream

In front of his huddled family
The blood goes everywhere
And they live with it
And the killers— shit
Something the Raccoon wouldn't even wash

Daylight goes
Evening is soon
My friends, we are to become
The last light in the pond

ANDREW SALKEY

Victor

(In Memory of Victor Jara)

Take a fistful of hurt;
trap a hive of shame;
hold a lump of loss;
knead them into song, again!

Ease the pain through bamboo,
true as lime, true as salt!

Break down the gates of death!

Demand the broken hands;
take back the crushed skull;
seize the burst heart;
make the song whole, again!

Ease the pain through bamboo,
true as lime, true as salt!

Break down the gates of death!

Heal the broken hands;
mend the crushed skull;
stitch the burst heart;
make the singer sing, again!

Ease the pain through bamboo,
true as lime, true as salt!

Break down the gates of death!

Love the words he used;
clasp the poetry close;
wrap the strings tight;
sing all his songs, again!

Ease the pain through bamboo,
true as lime, true as salt!

Break down the gates of death!

Press Chile flat as a bird;
slip it into the book of hope;
carry it always round with you;
sing it like a song, again!

Ease the pain through bamboo,
true as lime, true as salt!

Break down the gates of death!

Heal the broken hands;
mend the crushed skull;
stitch the burst heart;
make the singer sing, again!

HUGO LOYÁCONO

Victor Jara

an extract

With your hands making starlike sketches from the strings of your
        guitar,
with your hands that caressed the children of silence
        with the sound of your music
with your hands that reached the condors
and brought men closer to the sun
washing light into the smiles of children
with your hands weaving together in the song of hunger and pain
dreams and the sadness of all the children
with your fingers trapped in the shouts
and the blood of the people gathered in your hands . . .

You who stood tall upon the Andes
your bitter shade will come back on the wings of your death
tumbling over and scattering sweetness over the earth
and remaining anchored in all of the American earth.

Translated from the Spanish by Ida Langman

VICTOR JARA

Chile Stadium

There are five thousand of us here
in this little part of the city.
We are five thousand.
I wonder how many we are in all
in the cities and in the whole country?
Here alone
are ten thousand hands which plant seeds
and make the factories run.
How much humanity
exposed to hunger, cold, panic, pain
moral pressures, terror and insanity?
Six of us were lost
as if into starry space.
One dead, another beaten as I could never have believed
a human being could be beaten.
The other four wanted to end their terror—
one jumping into nothingness,
another beating his head against a wall,
but all with the fixed look of death.
What horror the face of fascism creates!
They carry out their plans with knife-like precision.
Nothing matters to them.
For them blood equals medals,
slaughter is an act of heroism.
Oh God, is this the world that you created?
For this, your seven days of wonder and work?

Within these four walls only a number exists
which does not progress.
Which slowly will wish more and more for death.
But suddenly my conscience awakes
and I see this tide with no heartbeat,
only the pulse of machines
and the military showing their midwives faces
full of sweetness.
Let Mexico, Cuba and the world
cry out against this atrocity!
We are ten thousand hands
which can produce nothing.
How many of us in the whole country?
The blood of our compañero Presidente
will strike with more strength than bombs and machine guns!
So will our fist strike again.

How hard it is to sing
When I must sing of horror.
Horror which I am living
Horror which I am dying.
To see myself among so much
and so many moments of infinity
in which silence and screams
are the end of my song.
What I see I have never seen
What I have felt and what I feel
will give birth to the moment. . . . .

Translated from the Spanish by Joan Jara

VI.   Bloodying the Twilight

RICARDO GARIBAY

Pablo Neruda's Funeral

The funeral procession begins at the poet's house, where the corpse was lying in state attended by his widow and sisters. The wake is held in the middle of a muddy, flooded room that was once his library. Books and documents are floating in the mud along with furniture. The day before, a stream was diverted into the house by the military, who smashed everything in sight with their rifle butts and left the house flooded.

The coffin has been removed and is being carried by some friends of the poet. Only a few people are present accompanying the widow and sisters, and the Mexican ambassador, Martínez Corbala.

Someone inquires and is told "Pablo Neruda." "What?" "Yes, sir, Pablo Neruda." And quietly the word spreads, and the name opens doors and windows, it begins to appear at half-closed shops, it descends from telephone poles with the workers who worked on them, it stops buses and it empties them, brings out people running from distant streets, people who arrive already crying, still hoping it is not true. The name keeps emerging like a miracle of anger, in hundreds and hundreds of people—men, women, children, almost all poor, almost all people of the shantytowns of Santiago—each of them becoming Pablo Neruda.

We hear a grayish noise of ordinary shoes, we smell the infinite dust, we feel on our eyes the strained breathing of thousands of throats that are ready to explode.

Then we hear a sound; shy, half-choked, prayed in secret—"Comrade Pablo Neruda"—and we hear an answer of someone who is saying, "Don't tell that I said it." "Here, now and forever."

A voice shouts, "Comrade Pablo Neruda!" and there, already in anger, "Here!"—already throwing a hat, stepping firmly and facing the military who are approaching and surrounding the crowd.

And here begins something that we imagined ancient and monumental, something from the realm of great literature, something incredible, necessarily fantastic, because it belonged to pure thought and would never appear in the flesh at a street corner. Some kind of giant litany for who knows how many dead. Who knows how many more murdered people this litany is for? A remote shrill voice howls in a bestial, heartbreaking way, "Comrade Pablo Neruda!" And a choir watched by millions of assassins, by millions of informers, sings, "Here, with us, now and forever!"

There, farther, here, on the right, on the left, at the end of the marching column, a column of three thousand, the Chilean cries rise up, twists of an inexhaustible womb of sadness, twinges of light: "Comrade Pablo Neruda!" "Comrade Pablo Neruda!" "Comrade Pablo Neruda!" "Comrade Salvador Allende!" "Here!" "Here!" "Here, with us, now and forever!" "Chilean people, they are stepping on you, they are assassinating you, they are torturing you!" "Chilean people, don't give up, the revolution is awaiting us, we'll fight until we finish with the henchmen!"

Swirls of crying, swearings, threats, wailings, of darkness at noon, of voices choking with anger. Hellish vocabulary, crazy heavenly words. Three thousand overwhelmingly defeated people are howling.

And suddenly, howling powerfully, a woman begins to sing Neruda's verses. Her voice grows suddenly alone. "I have been reborn many times, from the depths / of defeated stars . . ."—and all shout, all, they shout from their memories—". . . reconstructing the threads / of eternities that I populated with my hands."

Translated from the Spanish by Mauricio Schoijet

CARLOS GOLIBART

For Pablo Neruda

an extract

. . . The Generals had a field day.
For every hundred bodies
They got one share in the Copper Mines.
In the futbol stadium in Santiago,   beneath the stands,
They buggered each other to the
Death-cold Carabineros tune of 'Dispara!,'
While bloodied blindfolds were readied for others.

94

Generals' fantasies of Rome,
Thumbs-downing everyone, letting loose the starving,
Khakied lion-jackals on the Christians,
The Christain Democrats, the Izquierdistas.
Ideas mattered little to them;
Flesh digests easier.

What did it matter to the lion-jackals?
Who could match free medical and all the
Blood they could gulp down?
One could almost see them wearing the tricolored hats
Of the Old Guardia Civil Española.

García Lorca once wrote about the shapeless pistols
Hidden in their skulls.
The same shapeless pistols that would
Silence his physical tongue,
And would dump him in a callous ditch in July of 1936.
Was it five in the afternoon?
Was it five in the afternoon?

Yet Lorca lives today.
Like the stallion that escaped from the Sterile
Stable of Bernarda Alba, Lorca fought
In his poetry for the right to be a
Free Spirit in Spain, to dance with the
Gypsy woman, Rosa de los Camborios,
Without holding her severed breasts on a tray.

Although the Executioner, the Generalísimo
Still spews declarations of maggots from his
Falangist spittle, and exhales the breath of
Murder,
Lorca exists to ignite the imagination of
Poets.

Pablo Neruda, you too live today
In Chile charging the Underground Conduits.
Your words purify the air from the stench of

Gunpowder clouds, smoked flesh, and melted page.
Your 'Canto General' is sung to the Generals.
Muffled elegies to you are heard over the Firing Squad.

Please.
Run through the streets as you desire,
Shouting, with a green knife.
Pull down Condor Blue Eye, and cut off his talons.
Then watch as the Jackal Generals gorge themselves
To death on the vulture's carrion.

Bring with you "Juan Cortapiedras."
Bring with you "Juan Comefrío."
Bring with you "Juan Piesdescalzos."

And tell the Chilenos, Pablo Neruda, what you told
Your people of the Andes:
"Hablad por mis palabras y por mi sangre"
(Speak through my words and through my blood).

The Movie is not over. It is only the Intermission.

CHRISTIAN RIONDET

Words for Pablo

this difficulty of writing about
the necessity of writing
                          this
emptiness of vocabulary   it
is the visible form of the hollow
of the seasons at the edge of the tombs
where there are no more hands
that unravel the hair of
anyone
            and you
            weak light

haven't we sung
of flamboyant summers
                              but
                              let's speak
                              rather
about pablo
              who falls
                      in
the ash
        who leaves us
        with
this difficulty of writing about
the cruelty of writing
                          these
phrases that aspire
the life of words to spread them out on
the grayness of hellos–goodbyes
                              let's speak
                              rather
about pablos who leave us
                          with
this vanity of writing about
the cruelty of braiding a few
stanzas around their cadavers
because
          listen to me
we're talking about cadavers
don't faint in the
beauty of the lines
we're talking
about bayonets in the living flesh
and sexes cut off
copper and the c.i.a.
boots kicking in children's heads
and brains spattered on the walls
and the river carrying cadavers
          that's what it's about
cadavers, cadavers, friends,
warm friends of our warm lives

this difficulty of writing about
the stink of the colonels
and the transmutations of the dollar
o chile   o chile

                  o chile
the poverty of writing about
the difficulty of writing   these
efforts to get out of ourselves
bursts changing cadavers
into immortals
                  into immortals
                              because
cadavers rot, friends,
the flesh rots
with/without sex a dead man rots
dead children rot
                        this
difficulty of writing about these smells
of corruption/bodies becoming
gruel and then liquid and then
nothing around the whitened bones
o chile
            o chile

a cross raised by hands
clutching one another
and the ashes of books in buckets of blood

this difficulty/feeling oneself transformed
into swamps/dump for blackened bodies
into a country with lowered eyes
                              because
we shouldn't be fooled
and faint in the harshness of the rhythms
we're talking about gangrene
my warm friends of our warm nights.

Translated from the French by Serge Gavronsky

SERGE GAVRONSKY

what was written in black

men speaking in the streets
fistful of flowers
clenched women yelling "at last! at last!"
at the crossing the marks of blood

We stayed in the center of two men
staring at the balcony
somewhere inside rifle shots
the yelling never stopped

we move about in a silent procession
indians have learned to block their words
escaping
cars stopped
men in the country cry

so far
there has been little to say
a widow remembers
some photographs are retouched

at one time
something like uncompromising friendship
a single Yes like the sun

the city is reddened with sadness
uniform in its mourning
behind the window a souvenir
broken like unfed teeth

hear the agony murmur
that's what it was.
But you will remember the joy, before.
The cheerfulness before the suicide-murder.

Under the earth
where once they talked politics
and slept through their living room
a sleep now machine-gunned.

Chile, this hypnotic sleep
the machines pass over you
we wear black as print
and see arising from our eyes
the sleepwalkers who have begun again.

LIONEL RAY

*. . . it was from far away under the lantern that the shadows wiped
out the dignity of questions . . .*

land of hunger land of thirst land of blood with the hidden
seed of maize land of red germination land of fists land of talons
land of suns

here the dead alone are free — land sealed up! land of the
night! bare as the twigs the fire nibbles, like the age of the floods,
like the age of the rivers, like the wind and the face of the lightning,
like children at play, like the truth implacable

are there still happy woods in the world? are there innocent
towns? can one walk the streets of Europe without hearing the
muted footsteps of the Santiago dead with that copper sound in their
groans? can one laugh at a fete, look at the dawn, without thinking
of the frozen mouths, throats, bellies? and the blood! can one look
at the sea without seeing the waves at Valparaiso? and the blood!
can one knock on any door without dreaming of what must be the
hidden entrance to still unbroken courage?

*. . . it was under the lantern that the shadows wiped out the
dignity of questions . . .*

Translated from the French by Nan Braymer

PIERRE GAMARRA

Ballad of Chilean Liberty

You have opened up the sky of Araucano,
O Pablo, in my veins,
the gray ballad of wool,
the plains where the waters weep,
the seals, the sorrowful whispers,
the snowy bird people,
the slow amethyst rocks,
the parabola of the shells.

You have told me about the southern
cussedness of Spanish *romanceros*
and of the opal Pacific
and the rain over the pale reefs.

But this has nothing to do with knives
with bloodying the twilight,
this has nothing to do with the assassins
who tear apart burning hearts.

You have retold the story of the merciless
harpooning of the tortured sailors
and the red circle of targets
on the thighs of gilded men.
A rose of copper stirs
in the frosts of the dead gardens.
A Chilean with a bleeding breast
walks among the sails at the port.

And you have muddled me with absinthe,
mangoes, secret grains,
the mouths of holy madonnas,
the wise people of the forests.
You have given me steppes and savannas,
the long-lasting promise of the frost,
the myrrhs from the caravan,

Pushkin up there in the sky,
the land of ancient dreams,
orchids and black rubies
and the Cordilleras that descend
into the language of the night.

But this has nothing to do with knives
with bloodying the twilight,
this has nothing to do with assassins
who mangle burning hearts.

Translated from the French by Nan Braymer

HANS JUERGENSEN

Pablo Neruda

Many gutters have
run red threads
through betrayed cities.

Many trees were
hung with crops
so ripe they
could not fall.

O Santiago, you
too suffered the
staccato pitting of
white proud facades:

But your poet
has already seeded
his father's land.

QUINCY TROUPE

These Crossings, These Words

For Pablo Neruda, 1940 to 1973

where will they take us to
these crossings
over rivers of blood-stained words
syllables haphazardly thrown together
as marriages that fall apart
in one day

we have come this far in space
to know nothing
of the distance travelled
the scab fleshed hobos passed—

mirrors of our shattered reflections of
mumbling incoherent walking dead

in our red eyes the guillotine
smile of the hangman
the time-bomb ticking in the brain
the heart an item bought
the laugh a razor flash
the party time juba
of My Lai's screaming ritual
the pace a blue Miles Davis

& the blue-scarred wind
whipped rag blue squared with stars
that are bullets
& pin-striped with bones of peppermint
will not cover the coffin
of a corpse littered past:
it hangs there twisting
as a lynched black man's body
slowly turning in the air

of magnolias
over the blood-stained bride's veil
fluttering
as a flopping fish
in a gesture of surrender

& we have come this far in darkness
bomb-flashes guiding our way
speaking of love/ of eclipsed passions
to find the corpse of freedom
machinegunned down
for the honor of a name behind a word:
& what do we know of the roots of these flames
burning at river-crossings
the cross-bones of our names shining as swords
screaming as a Coltrane solo
the ignorance of these words

& there are times when we see
celluloid phantoms of no-legged lovers
crawling from the holes
of leering skeletons

still we stand here
anchored to silence by the terror
of our voice by the terror of the face
seen in the unclean mirror
& our sad-faced children
(who have also seen this face in the mirror)
walking shocked over snake eyes
of rolling bones that is the past

dragging anchors of this gluttonous hunger
& of this madness
that continues to last

NEELI CHERRY

For Neruda, For Chile

in the stadium the grass was trampled underfoot
in the stadium the lion was a skull handing out death
in the stadium men became grass
soft, underfoot, dark jungle houses breathing barely able to stand
and
for neruda, for chile
the laughter in munich beer halls
arms raised
and retreating to the mind's berchtesgaden to think to sort out
all that's happened.

in the stadium
      men women children
      become roses
in the stadium
      the true church dies
in the stadium
      judea is destroyed;
grass, underfoot, the last words he said to struggle forever

for neruda, for chile
the beer mugs full and overflowing,
whose arms raised
such a beast
out of the native soil
a betrayal of style
a denial of entrance.

in the stadium
his hand still sacred
in the stadium
her tears still clean
in the stadium
the voice still with us.

and we see
and know
and are assured:
all deaths
shall have an answer.

NICOLÁS GUILLEN

To Chile

I will go, I go, I have gone;
I am wind and wheel.
With the splendor of copper the world needs,
Chile, your life lingers in my light.

With an open heart, letter without envelope,
publicly I call you my earth.
I am poor, broken and poor.

I take your sharp geography
of dove and volcano, silk and iron,
blazing snow, and icy flame.

I take with me the tremor,
rain and refined summits,
the Magellan wind howling
like a huge dog whose bark has frozen.

The Copihue tree within its violet flame
gave me its familiar dawn, opening
from the white day clothed in flowers.

And with the wine I flowed
through the wide door
towards sleep-laden virgins of the soil.
Beside Chile my passion awoke.

In your body I counted the bruises and wounds;
I watched you fall and rise again
before a chorus of shocked hyenas
in the night trembling with your fire;
I heard the sea of voices answering each other,
as if I were a feverish and blind titan.

Next to the desolated offices
of the salt mines I hold the hard brilliance
and the workers' feverish gaze.

From the blind carbon to the dark center;
I saw the miner with his own kind of stone;
and he let me breathe the impure fumes.

Oh Chile, despite all I am a comrade.
Your enemy is mine. I go.
I am going. I'm not leaving you behind anymore
I follow Manuel, the executed one-man army.

Translated from the Spanish by Nico Suarez, José Rodeiro,
and David Rosenblatt

JAMES SCULLY

Toque de Queda

Already the greengrocer's on Merced
is shuttered up.
    Who cares
now, if he charged too much,
or that his thumb worked greasy miracles
        with scales

What few people are left
      are newspapers the wind blows

over and over. What difference is it
  what lies they told,
what stories
buried

That one, with the bundle tucked under his arm,
he was a child once
    clutching its pillow,
    his head's
        wrencht
over his shoulder, where the fear is

And the fat man with a limp, it's terrible
to see him hurrying!
He was not built for this
    but an easy chair, a sweet illegal
pastry: of sugar, flour, butter.
But with a hunger
    now
no black market can satisfy,
he drags and is swinging the leg
    as though it were young, gawky and flighty
        O so wild
 as never could get enough out of life

BOB HONIG

Did you ask for me?
Before I could decently make my goodbyes,
Before I had rid my thoughts of the machines,
Their private lives, and the meaning of the bread lines
Captained by the peeping, sooty children,
Volleying their new songs heedless of the tune,
I was as dead as the litter of gunshot
From my wounds flowed my blood
From the deepest annex of absolute desire,
Thick, like kerosene raging for a flame
To consume the banner shrouding my corpse.

Did you ask for me,
Before the strolling farm boys, lead over my body,
Milled me in the streets like raw grain
To feed the sicknesses of hunger and waiting?
Did you polish the muzzles of their guns with your question?
Did you knock on the right doors, a glass in your hand
Filled with my grime and sweat, a capital
That should have purchased more than the rope
Binding my wrists that had subsided with the final pull of my senses?

Did you ask for me,
Before I raised my hand, as though in a schoolroom,
To stop the tanks: I voted them their fair share
Of the falling sky blackened with their angels
Who poured my bones into the sea; happy sea
Engrossed in its own private laughter, rolling
Out an endless common grave into whose safekeeping
The eyes of conscience, once again, were given and buried.

Did you ask for me,
Before the affirmation of my own bullets deafened me?
The cover of bullets seemed like the tears in my eyes
For this losing of my life; because I had wanted to live,
Had fought to live in all the ways I had promised;
Kisses and dignity, the other sea of supportive arms;
Where a river of daggers had had its source
In debts and the shame of death.

Did you ask for me,
Before you were forced to sign the reckoning
The rubber hose had made with me,
You accounted me indistinguishable among the dead.
Did you believe your premonitions of the electro-shock?
Had they really mattered; only my steel helmet remained,
Snatched from the rubble of La Moneda by a friend.

Did you ask for me,
Before the telling of my race to the factories;
A stride ahead of madness in the crazed shooting;
Firing to defend the ground on which to die;

Before the fat tanks eyed me point-blank.
And the planes in their drunken swoop flew low
To whisper my comrades' names before the machines
Burst with the workers who could not surrender.

Did you ask for me,
Before the *poblaciones* spit out their dead like rotten teeth,
And mourned with their sleeves rolled, and the blue blood
Of their rickety presses running hot like the curses of old men
Trying to rasp their wiry, wizened truths
To the roaring presses of the proper giants,
That were never taught to speak simply, without shame
Or an inward glance into the terror of their own words.

Did you ask for me,
Before you felt that I had longed not to lose you?
Because even in your own agony, you could not let me die alone,
Because you still glimpsed the shadow of my body everywhere;
I was the crack in a shuttered window, I paced in the basement,
I was poured back into the same ground
That would muddy their boots, and stall their march
In the long-deserted evening.

Did you ask for me?
Chile, I asked so many times; I asked with my last breath,
Shouted your name so that you would know me.
You will answer me gently, my country.
You will study history to find my name.
When you remember, bruises and bones will have hardened
    under your skin.
You will repeat funeral, song, and your youth calling us back
With a loving rage for ALLENDE, NERUDA, CHILE . . . the
    earth's working people.

MICHEL CAHOUR

Now the night falls on Santiago
Unclean water beasts ruining the sea:
The sky is darkened, the earth is twisted.

Since dawn a child has fallen
The courier will not arrive
And the sky is about to die.

They have killed the song of the swallow
They have burned the sons of the dawn
And the sea, dispossessed, leaves this dark season behind.

It doesn't rain anymore in Santiago
The sky hears no more protests and the sea burns at the horizon.

The sky goes mad and the world shrieks
And the naked shadows dare speak only of death.
The earth no longer has a name,
The sea is deserted.

If only the earth were new again!
Flowers would blossom from the dawn
And the sea would tell of new perfumes and springtime,
The wind would sing in the light again,
The earth would deck itself again with flowers,
The sky would be reborn.

But the flowers have fallen
And the night falls
But it doesn't rain on Santiago anymore.

Translated from the French by Nan Braymer

ZÖE BEST

Neruda

an extract

. . . There are no sounds yet,
only tanks scratching
only shovels digging
only murals weeping in the occupied streets.

There are no sounds yet
but after the mourning,
whispering,
then seething voices
detonated by the Pacific's thunderwaves
marching the distance of the Andean spine
chanting the will of the Mapuche
remembers *Residence on Earth*
demands smelling all conquistadors
as dogs, as pigs
mercenary generals
blowzy emissaries wearing vests
with 40 pockets:
a pocket hiding a flask to kill ancient seed of ancient lands
a pocket inflated by jet vapor from aerial horses
a pocket with 10 million dollars folded
a pocket with ITT calling cards
a pocket stuffed with the WALL STREET JOURNAL and
     MERCURIO
a pocket jingling with copper pennies
a pocket saturated by a leaking bladder of blood
a pocket flat with xeroxed obituary notices,
         you died at the funeral of your mother, your daughter
                 Chile en el Corazón
Listen Neruda,
the seething voices, resurrected
born from the womb of your voice,
our future,
the future you blessed with your time.

9/28/73

VII.   Alive, Alive

WILLIAM WANTLING

Alive, Alive

Ah, Pablo. Your name so common, as
your love. Common. Complete. All-
encompassing. Everything delighted you:
a rock. a tree. a bird. a brown & wrinkled
face. a pear. a plum. a belt-buckle. Sea-foam on
your tongue. Your woman's smile . . .

O it was acid & swordblade, dew on a
blossom a spiral nebula the hollow of a
tree a leaping fish on fire, a god of
stone the State. There was hate, there
was love & blood but never an abstraction—
everything was concrete, quivering in
duplicity, in its tender pride & shame.
Even the agony delighted you. It was all
shining all beautiful, all . . .

Like the cunning crab of cancer (or was
it junta bullet?) in your brain

WILLIS BARNSTONE

Pablo Neruda

Who knows you? Lice that play
in the circus of your belly

or the mountains of your lean
country where the moon bounces about

like cheese flaming in a lion's
mouth? You make them: the terrified

nun and her shipwrecked lily, dirty
socks, onions, shoes, kisses that go

out in the street and give
away light. Those things know you,

me, us, and so you change
a few dreams of some lovers

and fighters, and you take wings
of the morning and go nosing

into our nightmares and the revery
of invisible agents. We are friends

because you and Sappho and San
Juan and the Chinese poet Mao

all keep babbling. You don't know
how to stop. Time means nothing,

you infect us like frogs bellyaching
on the sun in the volcano

and you absurdly persist. Your death
is horror because you are anybody

and death is good for no one,
not even an iron alarm clock. But

you and Cavafy and Tu Fu
don't understand time. Celery and mountains

of lovers know you. You give
them darkness and fire. Sad man,

you are dead. Not at all
dead. Hyacinths and your cousin's breasts

you hugged one childhood night all
say: you will keep changing us.

CECIL RAJENDRA

For Pablo Neruda

In the middle of the night
startled by your loss
I jump out of bed
and ask myself
What will happen to poetry?

Who will now
speak your fire, your words
your blood . . .
Who
will fill your condor boots?

I see no candidates
amongst the pygmies
who compartmentalise
politics and poetry

And as I pace the floor
between this wall & that
heavy still
with the vacuum
of your departure
once more
the blood of the hibiscus
floods my eyes
and I can feel
the crabs of despair
        closing in on
                me

ALAN BRITT

Pablo Neruda's Death

Dear Pablo:
   I write you
        a love poem now,
     although I know I can only make the sun
           pour sand from its shoes,
           or turn the moon into a piece of old wood,
but I have been told that every star
         will dream underneath the mud with you tonight,
         will sleep in your hair
     and hide in your knees
         that quiver under the rain,
they will all empty their pockets of spare change
          and crawl down beside you
        in the grass.

Your lips full of metal
heard the black heels click against patio stones,
they felt the flashlight's glare
rip your clothes
and knock against your bones.

My words fly from a thin odor
of two small bodies that cling together on the cold hay,
they burn their hair of frozen crickets
and hop onto your legs
then fall asleep in your lap.

     Your arms bow
like a violin
     left in a dusty room.

     Your eyes
       submerged
in dark water.

Your voice dashes through the humid pasture
    and shines inside a star-shaped yellow flower
        that grows beside the bull's dried dung heaps.

        My fingers
wrap around your waist
        of salt
    and pour you into a dark boot.

        Poor friend,
            the wheat made your blood
        hot,
            the rain
                dampened your shoulders,
    and salt always made you fall asleep naked.

        I wish to spread myself across your hands
                in that chair,
            fly inside
                that newspaper
    and kiss the apple
            on your forehead.

        But my lips are blue,
                yours are yellow,
        my hands are green,
yours are red:
    and they still flutter in the wheat's perspiring hair,
            they burn your shoes
        that run across the sky's broken ceilings,
            they are so hot
        they melt the moon's shoulders
                until its wax
                        covers your body!

The wind does not bury its torn shirts in the weeds,
        it must take them to the rocks somewhere
    so the hawks and lizards will not succumb to the cold;
surely the wind looks for you now Pablo,

it walks alone for a long time
                with its hands in the grasses.

        There is plenty of time for us all:
    a little goldfinch
        hops into your eye,
            a leaf
        sprouts from your mouth,
            yellow weeds
                cover your ears,
            we will wait
                until the hour's foot turns into lead
    and tramples our tongues,
            we will wait
                until the orange fungi
            reach around your head,
        then we shall reposition our bulky hearts
                made of wood
and have that long-promised conversation with you
                by the river.

PAT LOWTHER

Anniversary Letter to Pablo

That first time
on the moongravel
they jumped like clumsy fawns.
They were drunk in love
with their own history;
Satori flash lighted
their indelible footprints.

But you warmed the moon
in a loving cup,
in the thawing
water of your eyes,

120

you the man who moves
under the hill,
the man who kisses stone.

Custodian of footsteps
and magnets,
you take mineral glitter
in the cup
of your hand,
it becomes veins.
You own also the moon
now where they touched.

CHARLES HAYES

Pablo

an extract

today
an army
of words
died.

today,
love
trickled
with
death
and
hesitation
from
a
wound.

today,
wind felt
like

a small colt
stumbling
over its
dying mother
in a dark place.

i hear ink
churning
with death
in the well
of earth.

elm leaves
now bear
a rash
of images.

roses
turn green
with respect
because
they remember
the love
you gave them
with your pen.

birds,
trees.
even "the firm stone"
as you would say,
all kneel now
with cold brow
and leaves bowed
at the passing
processions
of words.

you no longer
whisper;
   'the wind is a horse
   hear how he runs
   through the sea, through the sky'

because you are
the wind running, the sea
and the sky.

down my legs
toward the floor,
i see
the two tired
bassoons
weep in two shoes.
they want
a place
to march
and annoy the laughter
of soldiers.

today,
a chameleon
felt lonely
and
a hundred guitars of
anguish
rehearse
even time
gained
weight
when
your
body
gathered
the
weight
of
death.

my chills
freeze
because
the cold night
is a soprano
of death

using my body
for lips.

crickets
broadcast
the final
readings
of your odes
as you speak
through the wires of roots
into the big speaker of night.

you are now dead Mr. ricardo basoalto!
i nominate you: GOD!
but now you cannot be God,
because you can only be
a stone
like the one that sang to me
when you were alive.

SYL CHENEY COKER

On the Death of Pablo Neruda

Your death has come to me over five thousand miles
while I was still mourning Salvador Allende
for whom you stepped down to present a United Front
against fascism and for the defence of the Republic
and the growth of an impure poetry (as you once said)

Pablo America did not swallow you nor the generals
who hunted you down like guanaco over the Andes and across
    borders
while miners and peasants kept you underground sharing
their torn ponchos and bread and the fever exuding
the nitrate and copper exploited over the centuries
how generously you sang them in the Canto General
the misery of a continent and people parcelled out

124

like loaves by the generals and colonialists who dreamed
of their banana republics peopled by serfs

And they hounded you in Spain, in Argentina
they hounded you in Brazil and North America
with its chilling hypocrisy closed its doors
to you while proclaiming freedom in the world
they shut you out they shut a poet out!

***

I remember you fleeing on horseback
over cathedrals minarets and the battalions of Spain
to the call of your destiny I remember
the ballads of the widows and the scent
of ceremonial virgins drinking your poetry
the only wine they had I remember your sad cancerian eyes
and the lover killing himself because your poetry
had become his lost sweetheart
I remember the hunger inside the incest-infested barrios
and the death crawling like a priest inside the taverns
I remember your great arms wrapped round the agony
of the poets who opposed Franco who opposed humanity in Spain

***

now you lie breathing like a permanence of parnassian gods
on the Isla Negra the flat-footed gulls
have come to sing you the immemorial dirge
and the condors always carnivorous like the capitalists
who dream of nubile virgins and stock exchange
have stayed away from the carrion at night
and the iguana is listening in his twilight

listening and watching dressed in your sombre verse
the great anaconda fearless and sad like your continent
unfolds slowly colouring the muddy river
with the umbrage of Sinchi Roca
and the fiery puma struck by the arrow of your death
has carried your message of flames to Hernández
Garcia Lorca and your great friend César Vallejo

***

I see Ruben Dario building the ruins of Nicaragua
as a monument to your immortal light
I see César Vallejo among the stones of Macchu Picchu
awaiting you to wrap your icy heart inside his Indian sadness
and others like myself little-accomplished craftsmen
scattered like seeds nourished by the sun of your face
mourn you because to have known you Pablo
was life spiced with cinnamon wine jacaranda
mimosa rivers alpaca ravines and love
but above all the verisimilitude of how poetry
remains the purest path to living and suffering life!

LORENZO THOMAS

Suicide Administration

(homage to Pablo Neruda)

We are keeping your file on the desk

The pink paper label NERUDA
Against the manila folder
A painted bathing beauty smile

Another file on a desk smiles ALLENDE

A memo blank
Clipped on the front
Says "Shot himself

Several times in the back . . ."

Here, at the Suicide Administration
We are overworked but efficient

We are only doing our jobs. We have no blood
On our hands

But these files
Remain on our desks

Gentlemen!
Please forward your last letters.
Then we can close these files

126

JOSÉ-ANGEL FIGUEROA

pablo neruda

they came, not to speed up
your death, but to slow
your life

            so, so slow
that no one would be able
to notice . . . that you

were even gone.   But I
               refuse
               to write
of your chilean greatness,
my warrior: as one who simply
passed away, instead, I will
scream feelings inside you,
scrap all that imperialistic

mud those soldiers touched
you with during that invasion,
& open new words that will show
fascism hanging by its throat.

Pablo, negro, you have gone
b e y o n d d i s t a n c e,
like any poetical bartender would,
               & your tongue
               will never die
               in one language.
some other bartender would put
your tongue in his shoes and lead
me to your path: w h e r e people
no longer mourn blindfolded freedom;
where one path is one child called:

         MI TIERRA / LA LIBERTAD.
Mother Nature's Fulano: you have

127

puffed new life in open wounds,
& like a child, i wait for you
to feed my hands and help me
to hold hands with t o m o r r o w s .

WILL INMAN

Late Chant for Pablo Neruda

Our brother who turns this earth,
speak in my living tongue
with sperm and maggots and sprouting grain,
with heartbeats via angry copper and hornet moons,
with twin earthquakes in Washington and Santiago
shaking loose those dread-kin juntas' jaws
from our common flesh, North and South,
O inseminate our song with fresh joy
and our anger with refining death
and our hunger with waking bread,
you whose magic cantos struck
jewels to life in throats and ears,
O Yes, I laugh, my Brother, for all the junta fires
can only scorch your songs into our throats!

ROBERT REINHOLD

On the Passing of Neruda

Along the Andes
Stretched against snakes
Of mountains you expired;
The spouts of whales
Erupted below Neptune
And the equatorial clasp
When your brow

128

Was hurled
Toward the Cape of Storms:
Rocks clattering
Over the Pacific
Made hosannas
To the aphelion sun
Of lower winter

You went
And silence
Washed that continent
Divided by papal calipers
And rejoined
In the gong
Of your words:
Music erupted:

A cortège of spondees
Moves up the spinal cage
Of Chile and Peru:
The rain forest
Is pressed
By the rush of your syllables:
Cockatoos and orchids
Roar between iambs
While the Amazon throbs
With drawn singing wires

Swash, nether continent,
Through the hemispheres:
Crash along waves
With songs of his passing:
Drift through Cymplegades
And datelines
With exhalations of sorrow:
Let the globe know
Of his love
And the final smoothness
Of those hands
That caressed
The planets

LUIS CARDOZA Y ARAGÓN

Pablo Neruda

*Tel qu'en lui-même enfin l'éternité le change.**
—*Stephane Mallarme*

I love the power in the tenderness of your anger, whether in description or synthesis of a vision, or some indescribable state of the soul. Whether you sing of onions or barbed wire. In your grief for the death of Silvestre Revueltas, in those poems about your stubborn love for Spain, and for our own villages in *Canto General*.

I love your Amazonian, overwhelming flow, the Milky Way you create of burning torrents and violent shadows.

I love the rooted link you make of man, his place, his poetry.

I love above all things that beautiful, central, and earthbound unity.

I love your love of liberty, of peace, your fight to make the New World truly new.

I love the spaciousness of your creation, which is not a single ocean, but worlds within worlds which unfold to reveal themselves in the golden coherencies of your work.

I love your fecundity, which is not simply extension, but the impossibility of exhausting a poem, however short it may be.

I love your prodigal and prodigious fullness.

I love your constellation, your endless mountains, and the incessant purity of your voice, which may not be curbed.

I love the sincerity of your poem about Stalin, as I love the desolate and impatient "Tango for a Widower."

I love your *impurity*, your lighthouses of hope and rich manure, of joy and porphyry, the breadth of that whole note your voice holds at its height.

I love the twists of kinship and passion in *Residencias*; all your books, with their accents of trembling steel.

*"Just as he changes himself, in the end eternity changes him"

I love your simple obscurity, your cosmic sensuality, your heavenly gluttony, your solar complexity.

I love your steadfastness, at whatever cost.

I love the limits and the astonishing imaginative power of your poetry, your poems of high plains, and of pre-Columbian hieroglyphics.

I love your fulminating anger, your smile of perplexed water, your rushing stutter, your direct, unceasing passion.

I love your black bread, your Archangel's sword, your granite and your foam, the green horse of your poetry, the rose of your lover.

I love your slow talk of boa constrictors, and the Edenic fervor of that world always dawning.

I love the excess and geometry of your crystals.

I love Whitman in the north.

In the south, I love Neruda.

Translated from the Spanish by Howard and Dora McCord

STEVE KOWIT

"Neruda's remains were expelled this week . . ."

In a pitch of bone
it is singing at night
from its Andean crypt
its rhapsodic, implacable
hymns to the people, its
loves & a lamentation
that rumbles up from the pit
of the land like a temblor
of music entwined
in the roots of the corn.

Wherever they plant
his corpse they
harvest his voice.

On the coast,
in the smothering beat
of its surf its
insistent note,
the disenfranchised
fish & inland the Araucanian
tilling the broken stone:
even the *generalísimos*
of the corporate state
with their medallions
& rings & executions
& surreptitious
assignations have
heard the news
that whistles up
from the bones
where they hum
in a subterranean wind.

Get rid of it! Get
rid of that thing!
that vagabond corpse
haunting the land
with its singing
seductive heart
like a branching
stream!

            But they can't.
Pieces lie scattered
over the uplands, fixed
in the rock at
Chuquicamata,
the loom of the fields,
bits have been washed

in the crystalline falls,
the puma has known him
at night amid the dark
leaves, he is in the grain
of the coast, he has mingled
his blood with the loam,
he has seeded it all, in
every apple you suck
he is singing!

Dig it up! Root it out!
Get rid of that voice
with its wallowing
freedoms!

They would have the lights
of the hazelnut tree
go out over Chile.
But they can't. They
can't do a thing. He
remains where he's been
& there isn't a foot
of the landscape he isn't.

Over the narrow tomb
of the nation the hair
of his luminous grave
is sprouting,
a perdurable sword-
like agave,
from the center
of which a heart
more red than the fresh rose
of blood, louder
than flashing copper
& glowing like dawn
uprises & blooms
& is singing.

VIII. Doomsday in Santiago

OSMAN TÜRKAY

Doomsday in Santiago

an extract

In the National Stadium,
in Santiago, though handcuffed,
I am collecting pieces of heaven
in this wrecked microcosm
as proofs
which the children of another world
may ask to study. For
what is meant by disappearance?
Is it the extinction of a candle
that burned deep in our blood,
or is it the disintegration of the sun?
Look how stars blast
and fly high above the other stars. Is this
the language of terror
or torture: violence frightened
mind and freedom—
bestial claws and jaws. Hope
is the world
which never shall be regained.
Chile is in flames now,
nightly Neruda is dying
in his own milky-white fire,
in yearning, in the yellow smoke
of his own books. Hope is gone. Time
would not bring back
the eternally lost Atlantis
from the heart of the millions . . .

Translated from the Turkish

EVA KOVÁCOVÁ

What's Theirs

Within all of them crouches hushed fear,
that again . . .
and perhaps . . .
then . . .
maybe . . .
Within all of them dwells the quiet of terror,
they are now compelled to love.

The Cordilleras reach up to the skies,
extinguished volcanoes, sharp-edged cliffs.
But mostly deeds touch the heavens,
clenched fists, proud kings.

The seas are raging. Blood suffocated.
Chile is fed with corpses.
(For truth—death! For light—death!
For a smile—death! For a poem—death!)
Within all of them a sense of fear,
what if . . .
once again . . .
sometimes . . .
anew . . .
Within all of them dwells the quiet of terror.
But it will never silence the sacred passion of words.

Translated from the Slovak by Anča Vrbovská

ELIAS HRUSKA-CORTES

El Golpe

The junta said . . .
   the junta / los hijoputas
      this day año de sangre
      11 de septiembre
         september 11th
            Allende is dead
            civil war looms
            golpe de estado
junta hijoputas
   the watergate gangsters
      the IT&T mob
         tear open the pulsating heart
         and drink the rich blood
            aun palpitante de calor
the golpe that defeated Spain
the monstrous victory of death
      the claws and fangs of the generals
   Allende muerto
      valiente until the last refusal
      tu pueblo o tu vida
   Allende refused to deal
      and died a hero
      and the godfather
         (nixon and the watergate mob)
         the ton ton macoutes de washington
         are alive and well
      and the generals suck
      their cigars
   Allende refused to violate the law
      civil war looms
         Allende está muerto
      washington sings
      and Cuba is punished
         on the high seas
         her merchant ships are hit

with fascist shells
little men with stilts cat-whiskers
and loud voices
issue forth mercurios
the official version of reality
the mice aspire to be men
¡mercurio!
baboons in santiago
monkeys in uniforms wear
swastikas and american flags
around their necks
and in the Barrio
swastikas and american flags
hold up the pants
of the monkeys with elastic caps
guevoless chiquita banana monkeys
masturbating blood into their ori-feces
in the Barrio, u.s.a.
in santiago de Chile
like Vietnam
Cambodia and
Laos
shall I write to *my* congressman?
or *my* senator?
or *my* governor?
or *my* president?
they not only eat chiquita bananas
they own them
like the oil copper tin coffee silver
blood
the blood
no not the blood
la sangre es de mi Raza
it is my blood that flows
the blood of mi Raza they spill
with their juntas
de mierda
the hijoputa assassins
the watergate murderers

wanted for murder and treason
                              / watergate pays well
          $2,000 per conference to hear the small-timers
          tell their tale of crime in person
northamericans turn the other cheek to
          watch the next episode in
          watergate intrigue followed by
          mod squad
              —the groovy pigs
          and dragnet with his pal tuesday
              —friday sold out to cbs
                 changed his name to quien fue?
                        tu fu or kung fu
                 modern version of the cisco kid
in the distance los tambores suenan
          tambores q. tumban
          cuero q. arde bajo el sudor de las palmas
          are they the bombas
                 exploding inside?
          are they bomberos
                 sirens screaming in anguish?
in the distancia the tambores
          beat like the heart of our pueblo
              beat corazón
                 beat forever corazón
                     but not defeat
                 late corazón
                     late
                 quema el cuero
                 load the popular guns
                 restore restore constitutional law
                 restore the republic
                     con la revolución
                        batista cayó y subió Fidel
                        con armas no con palabras
words are cheap
revolutions are weighed in blood plasma
transfusions
tumba q. te tumba en la distancia

golpe con golpe
blow for blow
the dead do not fluctuate with the price of gold
and the dirge goes on
otra copla pa la revolución
triunfa Chile
     triunfa hermana
mi alma quiebra como cristal herido
your cup is my cup
your blood is my blood
where shall I place my bomb?
where do you need my life?
Chile corazón
the dirge unfolds
     una mantilla negra lleva la viuda
     reina la luna
       only the smell of gunpowder
       dust clouds only clocks fused
       guesos y más polvo
washington monkeys gloat and grind the organ with their tails
new revelations
junta baboons show their raw asses
anaconda vipers twine black wreaths around
     their cocks god freedom and gold
anthropoids sit on skull thrones
     in santiago
       —end of round one /
       monos y calaveras.

Translations of Spanish expressions in *El Golpe* by Elias
Hruska-Cortes

el golpe = the coup
los hijoputas = the sonsofbitches
año de sangre = year of blood
golpe de estado = *coup d'état*
aun palpitante de calor = still beating warmly
muerto = dead

valiente = brave
tu pueblo o tu vida = your people or your life
Allende está muerto = Allende is dead
mercurio = name of the conservative party newspaper
guevos = balls
la sangre es de mi Raza = the blood is that of my people
de mierda = of shit
quien fue? = who was it?
los tambores suenan = the drums are beating
tambores que tumban = drums (or drummers) falling down
cuero que arde bajo el sudor de las palmas = skin burning under the sweat of the
    palms
bombas = bombs
bomberos = firemen
distancia = distance
corazón = heart
quema el cuero = the skin is burning
con la revolución = with the revolution
batista cayó y subió Fidel = batista fell and Fidel arose
con armas no con palabras = with arms not with words
tumba q. te tumba en la distancia = falling falling in the distance
golpe con golpe = coup with coup (or blow with blow)
otra copla pa la revolución = another song for the revolution
triunfa Chile = Chile triumphs
hermana = sister
mi alma quiebra como cristal herido = my soul is breaking like injured glass
una mantilla negra lleva la viuda = the widow is wearing a black mantilla
reina la luna = the moon is reigning (prevailing)
guesos y más polvo = and more dust
monos y calaveras = monkeys and skulls

MIKE DOBBIE

you fell from the skies / the last days

(for Neruda & many others)

waiting   on frosted lips
     bullets crack & hungry skies
   some passage to eat words
       newsreels of stuttered flight

143

alone   on crumpled flesh
    with sounds of running cables
no heroes   yet mangers fractured by noises
  telegrams of blood
    shooting across mercury vessels
    vehicles   with sounds strapped to electric clouds
    javelins of lightning in your eyes
      spluttered in guts of mud
        embodied torsos
of fulcrums tipped with the balance of rain
        firing squads melting into celluloid
   and burnt-out children
    screaming feet in armadas stained with tar
faster than madonnas
    mothers barking
  faces screaming
    twofold ruptures
  joint rip
    muscle meat muscle
    bodies float in paralysed streams
      & lacerated rivers in unidentified graves
stolen heroes they cannot repeat the names of
    streamlines dart in the broken city
      you will not mend them
    hills flushed with energy and blood
      you will not walk them
    bullets call your name
      you will not heed them
    they wait by fountains they have poisoned
with goblets stolen with forged gold of machine guns
      you will not drink from them
    climbed all amid legs snapped by the shriek
of spurs fixed into sides
      and platinum lips melted by poison
    deformed by curtains of paper promises
      you burn them
    boundaries of silence surround you
      they wait with baited jaws
    streamers of persecution

slices of face
stiletto eyes
you fell from the sky
beware of the wolf

STUART McCARRELL

For Chile
(Sept. 1973)

*"Remember Chile." Last words of President Allende to
Henry Winston.*

They were conspiring: the restless
snow in the Andes,
and the patient earth. Green
was about to break
in ten million places through
the crust of ice, fear . . .
The children were laughing more.
The miners were noticing more sun. Spring
was due in Chile,
a week, two weeks . . .
Suddenly death struck, demented, dark . . .

Now O beautiful tall sister
you lie stricken and sobbing. Now
in this terrible year of death
it is not the clean streams of the Andes
in your eyes, not the lovely white
milk flowing into the slum schools
you bless with your long fingers,
but blood, blood, blood from your mouth
matted into your hair.

In the slums murderous monkeys make speeches
full of platitudes and poison, and squeeze
the last pound of flesh from the poor . . .
In the mansions their masters revel—
all is diamonds, arrogance, paunches, fur . . .

Wait, work, endure, gather together
in secret, save books and rifles,
love each other, retain discipline . . .
Here in the belly of the monster
where your master's masters rule we too
work, and struggle, and remember Chile.
Always, always.

They can murder a season, a man,
a revolution. They can't even touch
Spring, or Man, or *the* revolution. Their days
are short. They have no future. Even
their brutal present is poisoned by guilt
and purposelessness. As each spring comes
they will try to murder it over again—
each year more hopeless. More green,
more melting snow, more books, more knowledge, more
rifles, more mockery, more life . . .
One glorious summer will find all the monkeys in cages
squabbling with their former masters.

KYOKO KOMORI

Driving Nails with a Rock

Kajumpa is a mushroom
Like the moon-shade surrounding
Santiago.
We must leave the property of
The absentee landlord idle.

We, houseless people, will have to build
Houses of our own—that's all.

Each man has a right to live
With our own hands we create the right to live.
Thus Kajumpa came into existence in one night
Like the mushroom that grows in one night
A cluster of clumsy board houses.
Deep in the night they heard the rocks singing as they nailed,
When the morning mist faded, they found the landlord's land
Teeming with human life.

The elders drowsing in the grass-beds
The hungry kids scattered
Barefoot in the sand.
Kajumpa is a mushroom and
It is the fortress of the starved.

Who would try to save the burning starvation
Of the people of Kajumpa?
Who would give the kids on their thin legs their milk,
Their eyes big with questions, their stomachs protruding?

When the wealthy friends of Nixon
Stopped sending food,
It was the Allende government that sent food to Kajumpa.

The people hoped it would be better tomorrow,
But they were shy
Eyes downcast
Ashamed of their abject poverty.

Oh Neruda, with your own kind of words
I wish I could tell the world
About Chile's tomorrow.

Oh Neruda, with your own kind of songs,
I wanted to join a resurrected Chile,
Singing together with them.

And now your voice, Neruda,
Is silenced under the earth of Chile.
Your brothers are victims
In the icy darkness of
A prison-island.

Now I hear in my heart
The people of Kajumpa driving nails with rocks
Without sleeping for a moment
Wishing that Chile could be known all over the world,
And my own heart is weeping.

So, Neruda,
I repeat your words,
Like driving in nails with rocks, I repeat,
"Never die, Neruda, even when they say you are dead."

Translated from the Japanese by Yu Suwd

ALEJANDRO MURGUIA

Newsreport

FLASH AS THE STORM WAS BREAKING
before the eyes of a watching world . . . one leaf fell floating in the
air struck the sidewalk and crumbled . . . bullets grazed the forehead of america . . . en septiembre when days are orange & yellow
& brown & red like the pool of blood that forms in the mouth of
Neruda from where a precious rose blooms in the middle of september /
FLASH TRANSMITTED BY A FLOWER IN SANTIAGO
it must look grim on the pocked face whore of liberty known as the
moneda that once the hit of the season before cara miada pinochet
took over with the junta of the mind (formerly employed as toilet
bowl cleaner by itt) pinoshit burro razurada pinchi hijo de un culo
that eats pies / pinochet . . . cara de panocha.
inside the moneda lights are out . . . radios are on and mute at the

same time the telephone talks and answers itself laughing about a
silly joke only the cia operator and his superviser can understand /
on this terribly clear day it is night inside the moneda so dark and
unknown that we must ask how a morning so bright a day so
promising . . . ?
there is an eerie stillness in the air . . . smoke rises from the pyre
of burning books forcing all living things to become stronger . . .
in a corner of the stadium they play soccer with the heads of men that
once worked and talked . . . screams of those condemmed will
begin at noon . . . machine guns chatter to each other like busy
neighbors . . . above the sts & trees in the air above the people &
the buildings above the guns and the passing jets above the city . . .
there is an eerie stillness of grey death in the wind.

JOSÉ KOZER

Death Is Pitiless

When it falls with Neruda over Chile, death is pitiless
with stubborn gaping jaws cracking out words
and a discreet warning that the poet has not yet been silenced;
while in Chile the Left is assassinated,
while copper is sliced into pogroms,
    and death stalks the stadiums.
Neruda knows it's a matter of people, he collapses drowsily,
his cancer pounded on by four generals,
pounding away from right to left, to the last agony,
their medals glittering from right to left.
The accusation I make is also pitiless,
it falls on the man who is against all men,
abominable from his bones to his outer flesh,
to terrify death. Neruda wrinkles his brow
and utters his most pitiless verb.

> *Translated from the Spanish by Willis Barnstone and
> Nan Braymer*

KEMAL ÖZER

If Chile Is Bent Like a Dagger

an extract

Hope has been made the target in Chile,
Now all weapons are aimed at hope.
Now the songs for beautiful days,
now the songs for days of justice,
are robbed of hope.
All weapons are aimed at songs . . .

The dawn breaking on the foreheads of babies
is banned in Chile now.

If Chile is bent now like a dagger in the earth,
if it is torn down and broken, it's still brave;
it will rise again like a sharpened dagger
to penetrate deep into the heart of darkness . . .

Translated from the Turkish

GYÖRGY SOMLYÓ

"Chile, when shall . . ."

for Pablo Neruda

> *Cuando de Chile*
> *ay cuando*
> *ay cuando y cuando*
> *ay cuando*

The drivers are no longer driving.
But bandits are all over the highways.
The vendors are no longer selling.

But assassins are murdering.
And if builders no longer build,
the Secret Service does not neglect its burrowing.
All this is so far away and yet so close,
that there seems nothing to say.
Always the same variation on the same theme
is the one thing history knows.
                                        When
Yes when will they call a strike against
the trusts and all the false presumptions,
the banks and the outworn shibboleths,
or Capital and its specialized commandos?
When will a great strike be decreed
against the highwaymen, the assassins
        and these Secret Service experts
                Cuando de Chile
                ay cuando
                ay cuando y cuando
                ay cuando
Alas! Pablo, when shall . . . ?

Translated from the Hungarian by Veronike Steiner

IX. One Circle of Light

OLGA CABRAL

Poem About Death

I don't want to die so many small deaths.
The death of somnambulists in all-night cafeterias
or clerks following their steel-file coffins to the grave.
The small funerals of varnishes, job interviews.

I don't want to die the life of AT&T,
The brain bland as gelatin in its brainbox,
a small electrode embedded in its gray crevasses
implanting canned laughter, military commands and jokes stale
              as frenchfries.

Listen: I have lived from Spain to Spain.
I was young in Guernica. I grew old in Santiago.
I tried to stop all the bleeding, to bandage wounds with
              petitions.
I tried to stop the blind bombing capability with my fists
              and cries.

And all the while what deaths! What grandiose harvests
              of corpses!
What chimneys! What soft targets! What magnificent madhouses!
And the death of choices:
death by hunger or death by the firing squad.

There are deaths and deaths.
There is the death of Kennecott Copper climbing 7/8ths to
              corporate heaven
as someone is pushed from a helicopter somewhere over Chile
for eating meat instead of garbage for the first time in his life.

You say this is not a subject for a poem?
That it is not even a poem?
That I should leave death to the professionals?
That poetry should be above "all that"?

155

Listen! There is a wind that slices iron.
The dead keep their accounts. The living grow stronger.
I want to die a little each day living the deaths of the people.
Bleeding because I am alive.

ISHMAEL REED

Poem Delivered Before Assembly Of Colored People Held At Glide Memorial Church, Oct. 4, 1973 And Called To Protest Recent Events In The Sovereign Republic Of Chile

In the winter of 1966 Pablo Neruda
Lifted 195 lbs of ragged scrawls
That wanted to be a poet and put
Me in the picture where we stood
Laughing like school chums

No little man ever lifted me like that

Pablo Neruda was a big man
It is impossible for me to believe that
Cancer could waste him
He was filled with barrel-chested poetry
From stocky head to feet and
Had no need for mortal organs
The cancer wasn't inside of Pablo Neruda
Cancer won't go near poetry
The cancer was inside ITT
The Cancer God with the
Nose of President Waterbugger
The tight-Baptist lips of John Foster Dulles
And the fleshy Q Ball head of
Melvin Laird
Dick Tracy's last victim

The Cancer God with the body
Of the rat-sucking Indian Plague Flea
All creepy transparent and hunched up
Stalks the South American copper
Country with its pet anaconda
It breathes and hollars like
All the Japanese sci fi monsters
Rolled into one: Hogzilla
Its excrescency supply the Portuguese
With napalm

The Cancer God is a bully who mooches up
Rational gentle and humanistic men
But when it picked a fight with the poet
It got all the cobalt-blue words it could use
And reels about holding in its insides

Do something about my wounded mother
Says President Waterbugger
Shambling across the San Clemente beach
Whose sand is skulls grinded
Do something about my wounded mother
Says the slobbering tacky thing
Pausing long enough from his hobby
Ripping-off the eggs of the world
Their albumen ozzing down his American
Flag lapel, his bareassed elephant
Gyrating its dung-wings
Give her all of South America if she wants it
And if she makes a mess
Get somebody to clean it up
Somebody dumb
A colonel who holds his inaugural address
Upside down and sports
Mix matched socks

And if they can't stomach their
New leaders' uglysucker French
Angel faces then cover them up with

A uniform or hide its Most Disgusting
In a tank
Cover it up like they want to cover
Me up those pitiful eyes gazing from
The palm tree freeway of the Dead War

President Waterbugger your crimes
Will not leave office
No imperial plastic surgeon can
Remove them from your face
They enter the bedroom of your
Hacienda at night and rob you
Of your sleep
They call out your name

President Waterbugger
Next to you Hitler resembles
A kindergarten aide
Who only wanted to raise some geese
And cried when listening to
Dietrich Fischer-Dieskau
Everything you put your paws on
Becomes all crummy and yukky
In New Jersey the mob cries for Jumboburgers
In Florida the old people are stealing Vitamin E

President Waterbugger only your crimes
Want to be near you now
Your daughters have moved out of town
Your wife refuses to hold your hand
On the elevator
Inexplicably, Lincoln's picture
Just fell from the wall
Next time you kill a poet
You'd better read his poems first
Or they will rise up and surround you
Like 1945 fire cannons a few miles from
Berlin
And History will find no trace of
Your ashes in the bunker of your hell

ANSELM HOLLO

Epitafio

for Juan-Agustín Palazuelos

Neruda
no feet now
in his socks
no living mind
in his brain
soon
no brain in his skull
but words! words! words!
in the world

thousands of words
in thousands of worlds
printed
       black ink
              on white paper
some of them
          possibly
              quite a few
(among them his ode
           to his socks
& their gracious maker)
still entering heads
thousands of nights & days
after the total
          destruction
of this
the capitalist
       oil
          monopoly
             chili
               world
in the long gut of time
in the sun's giant fishnet

TOM WAYMAN

the chilean elegies

an extract

NEFTALÍ REYES

This does not mourn Pablo Neruda.
I speak here the death of Neftalí Reyes.
Neruda goes on in the ocean of words
that is his life forever. Certainly he was stopped
before he said everything, but in that
how is he different from anyone else?

But Neftalí Reyes is dead.
He died of a cancer called The Modern Army:
a cancer present in every country. In Chile, in Canada, an Army
day after day is patiently training to kill.

That is all it is for. It cannot so much as make its own rifles
or run a railroad for very long. And it has no one to shoot
but its brother: neither an invasion of Eskimos
nor penguins threatens, and against the wars
of the U.S. or Russia what could it ever attempt?

Yet in each state, the President or Governor
keeps the uniform of the High Command in his closet.
Sometimes he wears it only on special occasions
but often enough it is pulled on each day.

As it was on the final day of Neftalí Reyes.
He was one of a thousand *chilenos*
struck down that day by the Army. And like each one
suddenly pulled into the sea of death
his mouth filled with so much salty blood
that for once and for the last time it was blood, human blood
that poured over his lips and chin instead of a song.

Neftalí Reyes is dead. But the great wave that broke over him
was scarcely a ripple to the sea Neruda
moving on the Neruda earth. Despite the deaths of so many,
the death of Neftalí Reyes, as with the lives of so many,
the life of Neftalí Reyes,

Neruda sails with his cargo of poems, with his freight
of coffee, bathtubs, typewriters, carpenters,
grasses, electricity and the poor: goes calmly on through space,
carrying the living and the dead
carrying the dead body of Neftalí Reyes
carrying the dead body of Neftalí Reyes

on the great Earth: pablo neruda . . .

(Note: *Pablo Neruda was the pen name adopted by the young Chilean student-poet Neftalí Reyes.*)

THOMAS McGRATH

Lament for Pablo Neruda

We may well ask now: "Where are the lilacs?" Yes . . .
And where now are "the metaphysics covered with poppies"?

There are vertical streets in Chile that end in the mankilling sea.
Up these the salt is climbing like a mineral snake on the stairs
Made from the bones of dead men. There are dead men too in the plaza,
Under the salt of the moon where traitorous generals sit
Sipping the wine of silence and crossing out names on a page . . .

You have seen the dead in the square, Neruda, and you have known
Those wounded lands where the poor are dying against the walls
In the shadow of Administrations, in the shadow of Law, in the hollow
Ministries where workers are murdered by the mere echoes of money
and miners are abandoned in the black galleries.

                                                    But hope is not lost
For you also saw the International Brigade as it entered Madrid:
"The thin and hard and ripe and ardent brigade of stone."
I want to believe you, Neruda, old Commissar of roses!
I hear your furious ghost calling in the midnight trains!
I see your generous blood staining the dollar bills!

And I long for the angry angel to rise over Macchu Picchu,
For the long wave entering the station where the generals entrain
                                                    for the North.

NINA SERRANO

Elegy for Pablo Neruda

You are dead
and what have you left us?
A voice that tells us, we're human
and it's
okay.
We have bruised up,
banged up,
lived on
feet,
and it's
okay.
We love and feel such pain from it
and it's
okay, because we're human.

Because we're human
we cannot allow ourselves to be oppressed.
Because we're human,
we cannot allow sisters and brothers to be oppressed.
Because we're human,
we love.
Because we love,
we struggle.

Because we love,
because we struggle,
because we are human,
we write poems.
We sing with our insides.

—Gracias Pablo.
Gracias a ti.

MARIA RIVAL

when he died

Pablo Neruda is dead.
My mouth is like a graveyard, without flowers.
My mouth is like the empty coffin when the ghost
is gone, there's nothing left but shreds of silk
and a faint stink in there.
I was hoping to grow old before I learned to fly.
I was hoping I would sing in multicolored languages,
waking up the ears of all the historic martyrs and
those people hanged for stealing loaves of bread.
As a child I was approached in the cemetery by policemen.

Pablo Neruda is dead.
Cats have continued to carry their paws ahead of them
like little fur gloves, indifferent to the passages of men.
Objects keep still, smugly, shivering when our backs
            are turned
only slightly, refusing to become anything.
I have heard voices coming out of the air, wishing
to console me. At other times people move their lips
            without a sound.
I never knew anyone, although I was alive for many years.
I seemed to be surrounded by emptiness. At other times,
I seemed to be surrounded by exquisite songs and
            wonderful bodies.

Pablo Neruda is dead.
When he died, things became clear.
When he died, he had made certain things clear to us.
These are the only things that have ever been made
        clear to us.
We began to notice the invisible nature of water,
and how, although abandoned, the cities continue to breathe
throughout the night.
When he died we were shocked. When he died we were not
        surprised.
We took trips into the public cemeteries, only to be
        approached by
policemen, and no one was willing to believe
        our unending tears.

I was waiting to be transformed.
Instead, everything has been transformed and I have not.
There are no flowers in my mouth anymore, it's like
        a graveyard.
Everything that had a color became a ghost.
Everything that was a song began to breathe silently,
        only at night.
I have been listening very hard, and I hear the noises
        of coffins.
I hear the noises people make when they aren't speaking
        anymore.
Cats continue to transform themselves into objects.
Certain objects which refuse to know the meaning
        of old age.
Everyone is unwilling to learn about my unending tears.
Pablo Neruda is dead.

STEPHEN KESSLER

Beyond Everything

> *"Ah más allá de todo. Ah más allá de todo."*
> —*Pablo Neruda (1904–1973)*

Learning the unknown road,
the steep one: five creeks
to cross in four-wheel drive
carrying neighbors home.
Helping to make the fire,
the carefully crossed
pieces of kindling; starting
a stick match off the kerosene lamp.

But bound
finally for this,
my house.
        Outdoors
the stars
have multiplied.

Warm enough here
but no woman
—sleep ruined—
the bed full of spiders
fears and longing.
        A stone
puts roots out
in the breastbone, beats
upward,
pounds like a moth
at the glass bulb of the skull

the sound
of new grief: Neruda
dead in Santiago,
of cancer—fascism—

his books turning to smoke
in the exploding homeland.

High in the windy spine
of the Andes
thousands, thousands of exiled birds
are sailing tonight like the leaves of ashes.

NICO SUAREZ

To Pablo Neruda

For Neftali Ricardo Reyes Basoalto

The spring already rambles
between his dry and forgotten
hands
and neither the night nor the lights
quench his longing

his twilight buried vertically
has set order to the silence
and a conversation of flames
and shadows,
struggles for his breath,
something like a corroding sun clings
to his body

he is the bell
contemplating brass in its quietude

the balance of air
on the arris of a dagger

"It was the scorpion's poison,
tangled lightning,
that burnt away his blood,

166

and his body
already drifts in a storm,"

but his last eyes
set the rain's curvature
and in the evanescent instant
his profile sets in words

for does one die
of the stumbled silence of one's heartbeat?
Is there not a more tender blood
in one's words?

For his words
are
a lagoon trapping
the looming shadows of the temporal birds,
for his song was human,
vegetal,
mineral
song of embedded emeralds
or wind, soft as flannel.

No, i don't speak with the burning silk
that anguish carries,
i speak with the foam of happiness
in its seed
for a man who spoke
meditating as a sky,
i don't speak of the water wreaths
that fail to cure pain
but of the quiet ecstasy
that Pablo's profile
gives us as a gift.

In his deep dying breath,
in his fine-eagled
figure
he spoke to us,

before his cold palm
garnered vertigoes
before the dark augury
of whirling waters
blurred and erased his movements
he had cut the passive silence,
had cracked the star of false hope,
and now that his body of clear smoke
is buried
in its sundown
his words remain awake

And so, why should we lament?

Because his steps,
steps of fresh and agile shadow,
persist in the spring's refrain
repeating his name,
in the torn moment,
in the deep hole
that his passing steps left in the day
in the light ray
sketching our faces,
there he persists,
exorcising nights
in the black fable of his wound.
In the liquid wind
that clothed his body
his moon hatches
clearings
in the bones of the awake,
although in the distance
in a faraway country,
silence has enveloped his life,

And so, why should we lament?

ETEL ADNAN

A Candle for Pablo Neruda

an extract

Burn a candle for Pablo Neruda
get your horse ready
we are leaving for the Andes

This city smells of jasmine
sewers run in its eye

I see you forever
a moon within its halo

One circle of light is the center of things
atoms are insane
you are the second
circle
expanding
and burning the hair of the sun

Spring broke stone
you are dead you are dead you are dead
I put a flower in your tea

young trees march behind
your coffin

I gave your body to the Arab
he burned it over banana leaves
in order
to start the liberation of the poor

Your backbone is a worm
whose head chews at your
brain
your kingdom is a heap

of words
I see the slow march of the night
in the eyes of the Indian

From the Mediterranean fields to the jungle
the banana trees are standing
blue like the sea
Pablo Neruda is buried under their roots
a man is always blown to bits
five sailors sing the Guantanamera
to a

dog.

Beirut, Lebanon

JOHN ROBERT COLOMBO

Proverbial Neruda

from a collection of Spanish proverbs

Pray to God, but use your hammer.
A little frightens and much softens.
Bread is relief for all kinds of grief.
Liberty has no price.
Others' bread costs dearly.

Nobody lives as poorly as he was born.
Every man is a people.
Remember: Eyes that see do not grow old.
Until the end no one is fortunate.
Dead men open the eyes of the living.
All good salt stings.

WILLIAM HARROLD

Musical Water

Last night I walked on water
and saw the face of Neruda
swimming sideways on crab feet
toward the coast of Chile.

He was opening valves, freeing doves
to fly their olives outside time.
He spoke through clacking shells
winding sea weed into sound.

"When Vallejo died, it was raining . . .
No one asked where the lilies were.
That day the tears drowned all the birds.

Beyond stiff feet and blackened wings
there are preludes in the wounds
of oysters, making the search bearable.

Light fingers trembling, the moon sways
above the keyboard. Tonight her round
white head is swelled with metaphysics,
thinking how many pearls to fill a dark mouth."

ERIC GREINKE

The Diplomat

(for Pablo Neruda)

The moon is an owl. It growls
& yawns. It greases its wings
against the rain. A blind

soldier paces outside an outlawed
cathedral. Mexico. Revolver.
Singapore. Artaud. A mantle
of banana trees infests the orchard
of the sun. A sleek bone twists
through a frozen crust. A star erupts
inside a lung. We stand upon
a cloud. Rangoon. Aluminum. Coffee.
Madrid. The land
is empty & reflective. The ring
outlives the hand. The map
outlives the road.

The key outlives the lock.

X. The Sky Is Red

DOMINIQUE GRANDMONT

An Example

I

With blood
for a friend. He is under your windows. He shakes
your window panes. He tells you what day it is. He tells
you the meaning of a single glance in a divided land.
Everyone's rights: abandoned silhouettes
on the sidewalk of Santiago. The child dragged against
the invisible wall. Women out in the September night
looking for food during the hours of curfew.

II

With, remaining in your hands,
books half-burned or else the weapon itself, with bodies
in prisons and their lives somewhere else.
With time, the outcome of theft. With
men tortured in the mirror of mellifluous and
limpid declarations: and the price of copper, for example,
or an *extra measure of soul* or anything else that is elegant
and distant, but which, in any case,
satisfies those who are not troubled by the smell of the massacre.

III

No. There is no room for the world,
"There is no wood for the coffins and no one to make them",
There is no news from the other cities from the frontiers of
    Peru to *Copiapo*, in the province of *Acatema*,
The names are still unknown of close to six hundred besieged people
    who are holding out in the *Moro of Arica*,
No one has heard anything about the peasants shot in the *Norte Chico*
                                or elsewhere.

IV

And Pablo Neruda is not dead. Chile
today is like a flower that has been cut
down where men gather, and those who
disappear in the crowd, in the heart of our cities,
and those who mark time without knowing it, prisoners of a helmet,
hoping against hope for half a liter of milk per day,
one day will read about it in the eyes of the women. Flesh
does not surrender. Crime
waits. The sky
is red.

Translated from the French by Serge Gavronsky

W. S. DI PIERO

Morning in Santiago

This then is the grammar of continuity
dragged into poor autumn sunlight,
cafe doors bolted, hoods on every barbershop.
Just beyond the city's wasted edge
the hours stop singing through the pepper groves,
somewhere the slight noise of voices
dying for reprieve, bills to be paid,
yesterday's wash still ghastly in the light.

In lords and badges and buttons and coins
is glory a verb for the present
predicting who or what is acting
and who or what is acted upon.
Lizards stop on the sidewalk.
Complex items are displayed in the market stalls,
images of succession and what will be done
to reconstitute, with one dry question
shoved between tin door and alley
whether menace is ever possessed of love.

176

We know what we are told, that flames
are guarding the palace from the past,
for all ideals are legitimate,
hieratic and savage, sucking pipes with good posture.
And for the worker no redemption
beyond the solid meal, for the soldier none
beyond his recent orders. No one whistles
while slugs bark on the corner, for this is a day
of order and palatable contingencies,
with old blood rising in sorrow's humdrum mouth.

CLARKE WELLS

for pablo neruda 1904-1973

the flies forage again, *las moscas sanguinarias*,
banishing, barbering, lengthening skirts, executing,
gangrening the long sweet land

father miguel died in the hospital too, pablo,
in valparaiso, after arrest, interrogation,
the unction drying on his swollen mouth

and juan alcina was found, outside santiago
without identification, submerged by the 10 holes in his chest
running blood in the mapocho river

and your library sacked by the robots,
last payment for singing long, and dissonant
to the iron clubs, the lace-and-chalice cosmetologists,
    the well-trained in tyranny

oh pablo, next time, next time
in the blind air, non-elected we vote with bullets, terror,
next time pablo, next time
for juan, miguel, lechery, the scattered poems

JAMES R. SCRIMGEOUR

Spotted off the Coast of Chile September 1973

Can't you see them?

the boatloads of bodies
    (shot neatly
      the bullets going in a straight line
      from the bottom of the chin
      through the top of the head
      so sweetly)
bobbing on black waves
under gray skies

Can't you see them?
the top of the iceberg.

EVGENII YEVTUSHENKO

The Generals' Boots

    (Telegram to a Chilean Friend)

    an extract

Where are you Pancho,
      the Jack London of Chile,
         my old pal?
A blow has perhaps struck you
        somewhere in the back
      like the point of a general's boot.
Perhaps you still hold out
      down there
with guns pitted against tanks.

You defend your country
            like a zone of final hope
but already the generals' clique
            soles ironshod like horses
brush your grey head
            like a steel press.
Santiago my beloved
            covered with wounds
the planes of the line remain in leash.
The executioner, exhausted, covered with sweat,
            cleans the blood from his boots,
but the reflection of Allende dead
            continues to gleam
in the black mirror
            of these boots.
And he seems to see me, Pancho,
my body,
            still warm, strangely warm
and infuriated
            pierced with stabs of spurs,
among the smoke-stained walls
            of the battered palace,
and they trample the ground
            thoroughly
                    to the end.
Like the spurs on the generals' boots
the loudspeakers clamor shudderingly
to reassure the people.
And the executioners try to cover their traces
            like thieves . . .
Tanks
blood of miners
            and blood of shepherds!
Wax for those boots.
And the country's flag
            is only a polishing rag for them.
And Pablo Neruda?
            They're not going to burn boots over some verses . . .

179

With the flayed skin of the liberty
            of Latin America, you have made
the boots of the generals!
Let each bayonet
            raised for liberty
            become a nail in the boots
                        of the generals.

Translated from the Russian by Nan Braymer

L. M. JENDRZEJCZYK

Migration

from the southern latitudes
swiftly they take flight—
a winter migration
on hunted weary legs.
men and women,
children barely born,
hands clutching at their
mothers' visions
of spring.

police patrols
track their spores,
and search out heresy;
trample the remains
of roses—
until they bleed.

still they flee
their new grey masters;
straggling across the andes:
a trail of questions
without answers.

can they ever return?
the winter rages on—
and between their trembling
fingers
are sprouts of green hope.

RONALD LEE EMMONS

For Our Brothers in Chile

(to neruda, allende . . . thousands)

an extract

They have killed them all now.
Poet and politician lay down
heart to heart, lay down beneath the earthquakes of Chile.
Soon briefcases filled with tanks and fighter planes will
wing in from washington, and the crowds will wave and welcome,
the schoolgirls dressed in amerikan flags.

And the people of my country will continue to argue
beef and pork; eggs and gasoline; and the people of my
country will wonder what this means to them.

While in the dead of night
the briefcases return, filled with copper and fish,
with nitrates
                    and warm human blood.

Michigan, October 1973

CHARLES CANTRELL

The Unbound Voice

He spoke from puddles,
lizard's feet,
the Andean shoulders.

From where it never rains,
or salt lakes boiling with copper blood,
to the toe nail—Tierra del Fuego,
where a dying tribe sleeps naked
in freezing rain.

He saw beauty unbound
by geography or aesthetics.
Dying flowers near roadsides,
rusty plows stuck in mud,
& roses in gnarled, grimy hands of peons
plowpushing grainward.
The poet always holding their hands,
crying together toward blank skies
during dry springs.

Now he speaks from a Gila monster;
rises, dressed in green leather.
writes poems in the sand
of a deserted hill near Santiago.
Several blow surfward at San Antonio.
Others, carried by eagles & condors,
scatter the length & breadth of Chile.

Poems are born in Concepción,
shimmer like jewels on Tupungato's snow,
glow on alkali rocks
in Desíerto de Atacama.

Though the Gila monster smiles
and retires to a lake of pearls;
like humble, hungry peasants,
we still accept the bread,
birth, & poems.

HARRIET ZINNES

For Pablo Neruda

If snow falls on the emeralded terraces
you have not seen the city of the Incas.

I have seen the city of the Incas
I have seen their mountain ravines
I have felt the ice on the lattice
and have climbed the stairs of the tombs.

I have counted the beads of the Incas
I have counted them
                one by one
And I wear the slippers of the Incas
I wear them
         down from the terrace
         down to their masonry tombs

I have walked above the ravines in the city
And have touched the stone blocks of the buildings
I have cut my feet on the angular stonework
as I walk erect
         with my slippers of the Incas
         indifferent to the depths of the ravines.

If snow falls on the terraces of the Incas
there will be blood on every man's shirt.

ORLIN ORLINOV

Chilean Fiesta

an extract

Oh, Liberty craved!
Cried with a song,
born in hope.
Paid for with white sweat
and black tears.
Then abducted
by a slashing whip on the back
still unconquered!
Sunny land,
stony land,
blazing land—
stretched as a copper vein—
you had the strength to say: basta!
From Santiago to Valparaiso,
and Antofagasta—
basta!
The vinegar glass overflowed—
the oil is ours!
The copper is ours!
The Liberty is ours.
Chile, you are all tremors and the rings of a guitar
under the delicate fingers of Victor Jara.
Chile,
you are a song!
Take away the kerchief, dolorous mother.
The agony has ceased!
Life will be an endless fiesta! . . .

Translated from the Bulgarian by Sophy Todorchev

184

XI. Canto

GEORGE AMABILE

Canto

for Pablo Neruda

Musician of stern autumns and whispering steel
maestro of the mind's muscle
your violet flowers & delicate storms invade us
like the miracles of an affectionate technology

Sure
even in darkness
you move along a desolate seacoast
your ancient head silvered by moonlight
and battered by the invisible capes of the wind

You are crooning to the surrounding night
in a clean voice full of surprises
the shy loves of rocks and hailstones
watches tomatoes and salt

On the far shore
men still shovel coal & dusty ore in the red ghost-light of the mills
  (their sweat shines like the oil of your poems)
women spread their wrinkled wash over shrubs in the early sun
  (they are serene and heavy with song)
and the children run barefoot through the shadows of century plants
  (their laughter cracks open like hard fruit and blossoms in the
                                                          wind)

STEVEN MICHAEL GRAY

Return of Son of La Guardia

it's the jets again
back from a hit show in guernica   they were
    dynamite in those
    villages, tore 'em apart, audience was

yelling waving arms high they were so
      excited so
in a surprise encore the jets return to a
         latin peasant stage & bless
them with the presence of electric steel, imported

to the proletarian skies by
benevolent missionary banks
to boost the lazy blood of the gentry boost it
right out of their skin.

sun-bathing christian demos in chile watch the flashing
migration of jets from the cold north,
the farmers run like chicken littles covering their heads/

silly fools, the sky isn't falling. . . . . . .
only the palace, if it's marxist;
only the government if it's antiimperialist.

allende falls across his desk piled high
      with plans to reapportion land,
give muscle of chile back to the
        bone masses, he
bleeds all over the paperwork,
the palace crumbles slightly &
stops. uruguay bolivia spain sound

silent spanish taps for a growing audience that
has to suffer another
boring routine of jets & tanks,
      the army's own

rockettes line up kick their chrome legs in the
bellies of the world & the mass homosapiens cow—it

howls & goes down, gives sour milk to the generals, gives
dented calves to the drunken junta, & gives

one slow eye to vigilance for the spanish bull that has been through
all this before, a
lightbulb bursting over his horns, babes at breast of mother running.
     (more poets crashing through retaining walls of
     night, garcía lorca then the
     heart that couldn't survive the murdered body)

picasso drawing it, asks the rockets to please pose in their phony
matador stance, they do & picasso

signals the hometown bull which has been bleeding in roman
     coliseums
for guess who, to
use his horns for something more than handle bars of the bourgeoisie/

but chile has caught up with franco & batista in the
pursuit of latin fascism, the latent mussolinis
muscle in on organized freedom—turn the
opera into a puppet-show—the

tanks are back for a return engagement at the palace of horrors

& chile can count on designing golf courses for
the rich & advertising
them in new yorker magazine. meanwhile

can anyone out there hear the faint moan of rice paddies sunk
by a hit-&-run truck,
               its license 1600 pennsylvania avenue.

     (*Written in Glide Memorial Church, at the Chilean
     Memorial*)

189

Poema Para Pablo Neruda

Traitors and generals of Spain
were in your blood-soaked eyes
in Chile, Pablo, and the shroud
of Federico wrapped your mind,
his grave murmuring dead children
beneath a grove of sad olive trees.

Years of singing and jaguars,
nights of jungles and coiled anacondas,
days of hot moving waters, of rivers
moving into the cosmos blindly
shot from your mouth like hard stones,
furrowed the pages of books
in an anguished hiss of meteors.

Cord arms and dirty shirts, stubbed
out cigars and dried glasses of wine,
cargoes and timepieces, elements
and cosmic tremors all thread your dreams
like acid and blades and perfumes.

Exile and more exile, ports and ports,
no haven for the restless surge of your mind,
Pablo, no assuagement of the terrible visions
erupting in storm seas and flames
all over the pages you held like empty fruit
in the gnarled scallop of your shaping hand.
The artichoke, the watch, the lemon,
all shone back at you from the gloom
like warped diamonds snatched from a cesspool.

Bed your bones in the pines, look out
to sea, walk down eucalyptus lanes,
chileno, in the stammering storms of flies
that feed on the rotted fruit of life,

and think of the grief you left behind,
rising like a cloud of white doves,
falling again like a blanket of snow
on the dead; the exiled exiled forever
and yet exiled, by god, no more!

CHINWEIZU

The Return of the Flies

Look! They have returned,
The flies with borrowed teeth!
They carry back with them the raping tube
Of the Lord of the world's flies.
They have rammed his wrecking balls,
Green steel without tenderness,
Into the delicious waist
Of Allende's America.
The flies are agog with ecstasy,
She writhes with agony.

With the borrowed muscles of the Anaconda
They have crushed the ribcage of Chile;
With teeth and talons rented
From International Tanks and Torturers
They have torn her skull apart.
Their slaughter is done; their banquet has begun.

For Kennecott they reserve
The capital parts of the sacrifice:
They lift her copper flesh to its fiery jaws
That delight in the crunch of metals;
They air freight her brain
To nourish the brood of its board.
They deny milk to shanty towns
And refill with worms and promises

The bellies of village waifs.
How terrible their smiles, those servile flies,
Carriers of misery to the many,
Assassins of children's hopes.

SEAN GRIFFIN

. . . And Gather the Banners

It has come again: the twilight
of the anaconda;
                    shadows
licking
the gaunt huts at El Salvador.
            And the breath
that sprang from hungry lips
swelling to a tumultuous wind of new springs
is suddenly foul—breath of the snake,
                    stench
of a visceral tyranny
laid open,
        choking
the mouths of the heroes
        and spilling
over the refugee streets
of Santiago.

And the generals come
utter the savage ceremony
                    apportion
the wine of terror
the traitorous bread
        and break it
for the communion of the corporation.
Brandish the hands of the carpenter
to hammer the coffin

for the crimson dead
    and heap them
on the altar of the predator,
their native land
      torn
from their wounds, like flesh.

The dead cannot be heard speaking
but like the grass:
    reaching
into memories of light,
Allende, Neruda
    the three years of Septembers
will stir the hope again
in the angular hills of Chuquicamata;
the copper-spring will return,
      hurried
by those
who hear the metal's bright anguish
flowing again to the oppressor;
    see mirrored
their manacled history—
and gather the banners
with their voices.

GIANNIS RITSOS

Chile

To Allende and Neruda

Raise up the beautiful dead man on to the walnut door.
Already the price of steel has risen 3-1/2 cents per litre. And iron.
Yes, iron again. The dollar. The boot. A pot—O give a shout!
a pot of seething pitch—shout out—for me to plunge my hands in,
    stupid hands

marked by the nails. Still they haven't learned to knot a halter round
    the neck. Raise up
the beautiful dead man higher over the door there leading out.
O bitterest fate, so many heroes we pass secretly under history
in the closed train with the cigarette-butts and the fishermen's empty
    baskets,
with the flags folded up in a thousand folds so that no one may
    recognise them,
huddled on the planks, all creased and camouflaged
like the bundles of decrepit beggars; and inside them a stone. Always
    there they sit,
the three blind dogs and the red broadchested guitar of Neruda.
A pot, a pot of seething pitch—shout out—for me to plunge-in
    my hands
that still have not learned to knot halters round the neck.

Translated from the Greek by Jack Lindsay

ROBERT HASS

Elegy: Residence on Earth

When my cat preens in dusty sunlight
the moth of her tongue
proves the soul does not exist.
She has never heard of Pablo Neruda
who knew more about cats than she does
and loved them better. She crouches
still as Buddha on the back lawn.
And he will survive as a song
of the tension in the distance
between a sparrow and a cat.
Maybe he will be reborn an olive tree
or a lemon or a nun who lives
in a little north Brazilian convent
downwind from the stink of the poor,

194

a girl who is watchful and quiet, who read
Veinte poemas de amor y una canción desperada
in high school and keeps under her pillow
a newspaper photo of Camilo Torres
beside the rosary she fingers quietly,
having examined her conscience
and omitted, with misgiving,
a prayer for the well-being of the rich
and the chiefs of state who are derringers
in the armpit holsters of the rich.
There is nothing to grieve for,
not Neruda or the girl, not the rich
who must tolerate, like the rest of us,
the elegance and indifference of cats,
their grace and shameless lechery,
and who, facing their mirrors mornings,
dream viciously of lemons
and wind in an olive tree.

DICK LOURIE

today

    (written for a memorial reading)

everyone who has died is here today
those who died in the struggles of the people
are here singing   they are holding our hands
just that touch moving through all our bodies
like a bloodstream

            those who died as oppressors
are here   they weep for what they once did
their hands have swollen to become giant
lobed mushrooms that sway like fronds   we sometimes
feel their cold brushing on our shoulders

those who died as babies and children are here
playing all around us in our bright rooms
and in the long grass   they are watching and
learning from us for their next lives

and they are here who died without making
up their minds as they called it   or too busy
those who lived like sticks   and never believed
they had sisters and brothers   they are here too

at last they want to put their arms around us
wandering among us they come and look
closely into our eyes   and they speak to us
about themselves   but there is no way for
us to be aware of their presence.

TOM SCHMIDT

Vagando

It so happens I'm tired of killing.
It so happens I see children clap with joy
for each new bloodflower the butcher draws
and I wither, like a snail made of water
crawling paths of salt and fire.

The screams when I shove my mother
down the stairs make me groan uncontrollably.
All I want is to stand up like walls or a radish
sprouting straight into the sun.
All I want is no more SLAs, smart as any Nixon,
no more moscas en el frente de Che.

It so happens I'm tired of Allende's last stand
with Fidel's memento machine gun, I'm tired
of Neruda, 'alone in the jungle, silent,
motionless in the rain, frozen

monument to murderous loving.'
It so happens I'm tired of killing.

Still it would be lovely
to frighten the FBI with a dozen red roses,
to kiss a terrorist's ear while it was full of screams.
It would be wonderful
to crunch through Sears in a tank,
blasting underwear and tv's and salesmen to bits.

I don't want to go on being a knife in the guts,
cool, violent, twisting with vengeance,
going deeper, into the warm shit and the bile,
thrusting and grabbing, sleeping every night.

I don't want so much pain.
I don't want to go on as a fist and a kiss,
alone in dreams, my brain a city of suicides,
Altitude: 6 feet, Population: 0.

That's why Friday, when it sees me coming
with my fishmonger's face, turns blue like alcohol,
and it slides on by like a cloud in the dark,
leaving pale footprints in the nighttime.

And I follow it into busy streets, open doorways,
into cantinas where faces get broken with rifle butts,
into subways that smell like graphite,
into automobiles that smash themselves against trees.

There are dollars blinking and cows grinning
above the doors of houses that I hate,
and there are hypodermics lost under bathtubs,
there are grey faces
that should have smiled, even once,
there are footballs everywhere, and beers, and curling fingers.

I walk cool, with my hair, my clarinet,
my pugnaciousness, my—I can't remember.

I walk by, through clumps of violets and circles
that the police cinch tighter and tighter,
through backyards dazed with carpets,
the seats from some old sedan hawking up slow mouthfuls
of bitter grey stuffing.

XII.   Tomorrow's Sun

WALTER LOWENFELS

For Pablo Neruda

His lost eyes don't show it
    but they cut a wedge out of his heart
in the Andes Mountains.
    They cut the shore line at Talcahuano.
They let the blood from his veins
    run into the Pacific Ocean.
They cut Valparaiso from Santiago
    but they could not cut his heart out of Chile . .
He is one heart, one hand for you
    one voice for you
O brothers and sisters of long life
    and your own land in Chile.

NATHANIEL TARN

At Gloucester, Mass., After Foreign Travel

For P. N.

At Gloucester, Mass., after foreign travel,
Labor Day mists
    the lovely breath of one more summer dying out
the sea
    swelled contrapuntally as we swam
and a smell of old furniture came up from the water
        into the dusting sunlight

As if all the woods that had gone down into the sea
        surfaced to farewell summer
the boats crossed and crisscrossed over the drowned
        and the great feast of work

crimson with lobster shells, stubbed toes and girls' bandannas
             set round the pink of nipples
in loose red shirts / O flag of love over America the damned!

We went down to the sea
all the poets together
and gave ourselves up to the waters
             in various positions of loss:
I realized that I have never dived into water
             and within five minutes
after giving myself completely to the wave

             I did about ten things
never done in my life before
such as: throwing my body like a javelin into the waves
spreading myself like a banner on the swell
somersaulting in the deep
holding the sand's thighs in my hands
             and all the fear was gone

We had spent the whole day looking for loons and grasses
old Dogtown had risen for us from the ground
and Olsen's floor and windowboards full of dates
had defied the policy on National Monuments—
    white building slats among the red stripes
             the stars on my Union Jack
exclusive to the night:

             and she seen rightly
had no need to be touched
             she seen rightly
became a thousand faces one after another
             seen rightly
there was no face the world could take on which was not her face
             and a golden aura
red with cheap scents raved round her hair.
             Oh the hands that went out
the bodies that moved out towards her on our belief
             Labor Day, Gloucester, Mass.,

oh the copulations that took place towards her on the arrow of sight
    drawing no flesh at all
out of its sheathing!

        The America he dreamed never existed,
        cause of lost causes—
        but dreamed it with the throat of need
        the passionate thirst of a tramp
        sweat on his whiskers.
        And she in whose hands lies my life
        brings her creased eyes to town
brings her body like a banner
she said she could not use
    advertising ships, and land, and whispers among hutments,
and "today", she said, "today,"
    "tears of blood coming out of the ground
at what has become of this Republic
        which was to be the laughter of the world!"

If it be true / that this polity
has killed Allende for instance / has killed Neruda
if it be true that Spain is being repeated—billed to this polity—
        then the devices of the world of ice
the hanging in the maws of the old windmill the great Giver devised
        shall be but as childsplay to what awaits
our shabby emperor in his greasy feathers -/-/-

        encore une fois le refrain

Swallow on the air
mackerel in the sky
mackerel in the water
swallows on the sea
        stitching silver to silver
in the heart's water:
        I am so glad to be home!

        I have laid up a world of words
for the immortal gods of this Republic

that all the 50 stars might sing in unison together!
      Our moods of love
as they will seize and shake us all our lives
wood rising from the sea, trees soaring on first shores—
      the Adam-hut, its ghost,
      I am so glad to be home!

SHARON BARBA

For Pablo Neruda

I was looking
    for a woman
who was also
    a poet
when I stumbled
    against your thighs:
white and eloquent
yet solid as the knots of trees
sturdy as
    the heft of your songs
You suggested
    I take my socks off
like a man,
poetry beginning
    and ending
in the feet
the roots
    or chains
around the ankles
poetry beginning and ending
with the calves of a man
    the thighs of a woman
the big legs of the poet

JOSÉ RODEIRO

The Cube-Root of Pablo

Dedicated to David S. Rosenblatt

Just before the comet passed, Chile
With clear nocturnal bursts
Without the sea, the earth, the wind
Astral mermaid's hair entered his filaments,
Vertiginous bleeding his blood's dark scum
And foam between the spiral mountain road
And the snowcapped coral reefs of his teeth
And his coast line that smiles forever
From each bay spinning the fibers of a moon
That also smiles with his unobscure melting
Skeleton of clouds, jellyfish, and Indian
Women who comb the night away.
All Chile was smiling with his smile
On every mouth. While Indian flutes
Played birds and bleeding coral rocks in
Your heart; all Chile laughed a thousand
Hands banging on one tiny toy piano,
"Write faster, will the work ever be done?"
Before a ship filled with "Pablo's" comes.
Taking that complete and selected collection
Of that one piano note from a toy piano
Phidias imprisoned in Athens, your
Aging Buonarroti had he to do it again,
Said, "He'd not be God, for himself nor
For us." Incessant enjoyers of the marble
Of the things sculpted like the dawn or dusk
Free, marvelous, a monument by anyone
Of you, never more you, anymore you,
Never to you anymore a monument by anyone
Who felt anymore than you of the seasons,
The planets, and the people who are able to be the trees,
Of the trees who are able to be the mountains
That are the orphans you left hanging and dangling

On the key chain that opens the door
To a slim and slender death with elaborate
Wings of mud, dust, worm, lamp, the music
Of the stars blossoming like fields of lost ships
And sprouting groves of short lances
Filled with short daily lives, the white marble cup
From which no one drinks which holds your eyes
While three "Pablos" left the shore
Adorned without assurance
The salt fed the ocean with the thunder
Of their bones, iron clad wharves
Burned behind their voyages
While shrines are placed over them,
Young frogs brood lighted in sacred shadows
Waves of unseen salt beckon the unseen savor . . .
They depart from different ports
At different times and sail
On the same ship upon the
Same land, ocean, and wind
Goodbye Provence
Goodbye Chile
Goodbye Catalonia

VINCIUS DE MORAES

Natural History of Pablo Neruda

an extract

Itapoa, Bahia, October 1973

Be seated there, poet, you who are older than I,
On this broad chair, facing the world
Let me paint your portrait
(Since your friends Picasso and Di Cavalcanti can't do it,
Due to circumstances),

In words covered with the verdigris
Of time, with the sea-green gleam of the moon
Erratically wandering between the hemispheres,
Detached from the skin of Matilde
Toward the "formagadiens" of the Bay of Bahia,
It is the dawn, brother, and I hear the sea
Murmur verses on the sands
Of Itapoa, it weeps at your death,
You who loved it, fierce as it is in its imprecations,
Like the black reefs of the Isla Negra.
So, Pablo: let me read on your face
The great fish of deep waters
And the little childish eyes
Of an ironic sleeping whale,
In your grave yet attentive rest
Of an ancient salamander endowed with prescience,
This near-smile of one who,
A magician, with a quick gesture, extracts from his ear
Slowly, a carrot, and who sees it, as he gnaws at it,
Fly away, changing into a dove,
Who rises slowly in the air and suddenly
By transcendence into the sky lighting up his star.
Protect your massive body (maybe there will be)
An elephant (the only thing the illusionist lacks)
And think of your shellfish
Of the beautiful scarabs of Africa,
Of the subtle and rainbow-colored stones.
Your collection of old ladies' boots,
Your starfish and your sextants,
Your sailmakers captive in bottles,
Your bottles of all origins,
Your prow heads and your shells,
Your horses (from Troy or Temuco?)
Objects that the earth and the waters have yielded to you,
    Sparkling, opaque, translucent,
That merge their unheard harmonies
Each time you look at them
in the cold dawns of Isla Negra,
Before diving, an enormous seal,

207

Into the luminous aquarium of your room,
And, with the fingertips of a blind man, reading Braille,
And then releasing from the empty air a new poem.

*Translated from the Portuguese by Nan Braymer and
Charles Dobzynski*

DAVID MARTINSON

South Wind in October

> *on hearing of Neruda's death on a warm day in Northern
> Minnesota*

To die before the snow
   the trees full of girls
   beautiful girls
   who marry the desert with the sea
   who laugh and leave
   and among them all
   not one who comes into the house

Alone in the house
   surrounded by prairie
   salt sweating in the wind
   wind that blows one blast from the south

I praise the wind
   it is the song sung by stones
I praise the house
   it is the stone surrounded by song

Song that rises from wells
   and more
Joy of beavers chewing ash
   and more
Sorrow of needles that sew the hunter's wound by firelight

there
to be sung
    it calls the ambery geese to sleep
    in the milky river
    it calls the mushroom ring into the driveway at dusk

    it inhales and exhales
    both river and geese
    mushroom and road

All my life I heard this song
    moving in and out of the window at dusk

Southern wind in October sings it now
    to die before the snow
    the girls carried off by flies
    the flies carried off by wind
    the wind carried off by snow
    the snow carried off by song

ANN DU CILLE

For Your Preservation

a love poem for Pablo

the day you died
I wrote a romance for your preservation
elegizic pentameter
as if you were my lover
lost
in the Public Wars of Patagonia
(or such)

it was a lie
        la poema

I have never known your breath between my teeth
felt your flesh fuse to mine

yet
lying here
naked
breast bare
between the leaves of your life
                                                    this humus
I make love to Macchu Picchu

and
listening with your eyes
I turn into your shadow
                              su sombra
                                        su sangre

seduced by the semen of your metaphor
I bear for you another poem
another
for your preservation

EDUARDO ESCOBAR

Goodbye to Neruda Without Raising My Hand

I hated Pablo Neruda—but I can't now—
now that he's gone like Salvador
I can't hate him without saying goodbye first
Chile for the moment
does not feel like singing and has no singer
It doesn't matter
there will always be poets in the world
running after words—some limping
and others faster than frozen Marathon athletes
sweating red

Everything gets old
and poets too have a right to rest
after the dog days
I hadn't read you for a long time
—Pablo—I should admit it
a bit tired of your kindly sentimental crust
and your postures of a crowned proletariat
and your melancholy of the poor wandering ambassador
But you won't read this poem either
that your death has got me to do
You have closed all the books—and your eyes
Now you will be stationed in Isla Negra
dreaming that death is a lie
and that a coffin is a black ship
steered by some black cock
Pinochet don't touch this corpse
Chile cut you to death like lightning
Goodbye—Neftalí with your sad swamp shoes
Go suck onion roots
and go peacefully
The world goes on spinning
goes on full of big and small poets
inventing the nation of exile
It's hard today to be a revolutionary
Today with revolutionary systems of merchandizing
Now it's good they broke your wings—Neftalí Reyes
and you enter night
and silence
that was always the nation of the poem
and where all poets begin
Today—I forgive everything—and that's good
not that you can add anything to your glory
Goodbye—then-Neftalí—·Pablo Neruda
singer of tomatoes and intimate friends of the harsh sea
and snows
Keep room for another return—if possible
—hold on to your sword
Chile is a sad thing
And America Latina is battle

Go—Pablo Neruda and forget politics
and its bastard general sons
on a bloody pedestal
Rest finally
Sleep as night trains slide by
rattling on dream rails
Forget your body
Let eternity knot your scarf
Here you are not forgotten
Here war goes on—parallel
to the marching sun that like you
was always Communist
Now you are a stopped watch a closed door
—a girl deserted at the edge of her crying
You are an immense plate
on a black cloth
But nothing matters to you
Death has its advantages
Now you've ended the list of your loves
You won't have to spell out the causes of your hatred
Nor—grinding your teeth—put up with injustice
Cancer liquidated your deeds
and the rest is something for readers
All is yesterday
and even tomorrow is yesterday
And at bottom—Pablo—if I've warred with you
in the back rooms of the soul
it was to shield me from your three hundred pounds of tenderness
and your Yonoguí face
and your sign of a witchdoctor ox under the meridional sun
and you were no longer—friend—Neftalí Reyes—Pablo
Now I tell you goodbye
without raising my hand
And have a fine trip!

Translated from the Spanish by Willis Barnstone

FRANZ DOUSKEY

Amorphous Water

they have taken the poet's hand
and chained it to the bed of the ocean
where he dreams of blood

he was standing by the window
looking across the ocean
when the lights went out

when the lights went out
the people pretended to be asleep
but the heart of the poet stopped

the poet dreams of the stars
at the bottom of the ocean

the poet's body is empty

if you hold it to your ear
you will hear the ocean

you will hear how a man sounds
as his life leaves his body

it is an old song you will never forget

EDWIN HONIG

Pablo Neruda

Under reason and steel grows the final poem of your death
in the city where you were the house of your breath,
smoked out, ransacked, squandered in shreds,
as under the stones precise on the heights
you guessed they had buried the rage of slaves.

As under the seal of wax there clacked
in the general's beak the white-tongued admiral,
giving the acid word of steel in the guts
to your guarded brightness, Life, with its shadow
invisibly wearing away the heaviest stone.

In your light blatant or hidden forever
under the everyday sky exposed
like a maundering madman mocked into meaning;
because no one can bear the darkness alone,
because no one can go on shielded alone,

Your name went up in the half-light that day,
like smoke lolling up from the cannon's mouth,
from house after house and cell after cell,
to show where the flowering multiple death
had departed your body, your country, its ghettos

As your life's first day is destroyed in the last,
as the mouth of the serpent swallows its tail,
as the spirit's skyscraper's consumed in a rose,
let all darkness be broken like bread among brothers,
all being more and less than a metaphor.

DARCY GOTTLIEB

Come, Neruda, Come

Come, Neruda, come.
Tweed me, sieve me
ignite my dream-swamp
with green fire,
braid opposites
with cords of electricity.
Cut me open
as at an Aztec ritual,
and wild urges
will spurt against
the blood of your thought.

I seek beginnings.

Neruda, you have always
been singing in me.
I too make love
to insolent life.
Now I would peel away
the skin of this onion-world
and return to where
the invisible, the pure,
mouth silence.

Come, Neruda, come.
I call on you.
Make me a revolution.
Reel me on the spit
in the fire of your worlds.

BARBARA A. HOLLAND

The Insane Pursuit of TíoPablo

Someone's fingers were always
among the pickles
in the big glass jar.

Someone was always trying
to make off with as much
that lived of him as was possible
before he could be gracefully forgotten.

Someone's curiosity was never
too sleepy to lie awake
in bed between two lovers.

Someone's lamp burned late
in the evening, eating out hours
of his existence with the caustic
of frivolous evaluation.

Someone even tried to pick
his soul from the laughter he became
when death salted down
all of it in typescript
and in foolscap jottings.

And when government fingers,
pen knives and shears
harried manila envelopes without
official blessing, in case one
undergrown animosity had fallen from
it progenitor on his return
to the waste spaces of Hispanic perversity,

and had stayed on as a flea
in the scruff of despotism,
even posterity would allow
no privacy to Tío Pablo.

SUSAN GRATHWOHL

For Pablo Neruda

(1904-1973)

"Conservo un frasco azul,
dentro de él un oreja y un retrato . . ."*

It is September:
We are bringing the garden inside.
Carrots bulge asymmetrical,
dwarf genitals,
pinkies and thumbs. Eyes
of potatoes bud underground.
This year, an embryo
kicks and hiccups in my belly,
becomes human. Once it was a tadpole
and I a river flowing through the living room.

In Chile by September, families
queue up in darkness for food.
By daylight, hijacked trucks
roll the loads of produce in.
A woman says, "We lack bread, oil and
revolution. We can do without
the bread and oil."
Last year, the wild cells
spread through my father's lymph nodes,
fed on his lungs and blood. He saw
himself dying. The military junta
"issues a restrained
statement of condolence,"
but thousands come out of hiding
for your funeral; a community
grieves through the streets of
Santiago for "Neruda y Allende
un solo combatiente"; its voices
keen, "We are burying Allende now,"

---

* "I keep a blue bottle, / inside it, an ear and a portrait . . ."

risk prison to sing
the "Internationale."

I keep a blue bottle,
inside it, an ear and a portrait

Your poetry
is vision
"born in the petrified cinder";
so I watch ears of corn
split their husks, shrivel
the green silk
dark and pubic;
so I see a metal bowl on the table
glitter in sunlight—cherry tomatoes
yellow and ripen, egg cells.

In the picture of the prison camp,
the people, Marxists,
stand in single file on an island
in the Straits of Magellan.
The guard's thighs, huge
gun and holster overpower
the viewer. The prisoners
recede down the hill, the most distant
the shadows of barbs on a wire.

In the distance, mountains
well up, ridge upon ridge, razorback,
waves poised before breaking.
Break, they will break
under "wheels that have crossed long and dusty
distances with their mineral
and vegetable burdens."
Whatever grows
first is hidden—
In the South, hunger;
in images of birth and harvest,
the possibility of revolution.

I teach your poems in August
to high school teachers.
I am six months pregnant.

At sunset I bring lettuce in,
Boston, endive, iceberg;
mud runs from their root hairs
through my fingers: I track it
across linoleum, through dust, scraps
of catfood shaped like stars, strands
of hair. Before class, I run off copies
of your poems on the mimeograph machine—

Printing fluid ticks into the metal cylinder;
blank pages revolve around the drum
and pile in the hopper, imprinted
with your images, "an ear and a portrait."
I hand them out in class, my fingers
smeared with purple ink. The baby
kicks inside me: we grow, connected
with the possibility
of revolution.

GABRIELA HARINGOVÁ

For Pablo Neruda

Out of the conscience of money,
out of the drudgery of mountain shepherds,
out of the rivers of Chilean women's tears,
out of the calloused hands of men,
out of the raging sea
and out of the silence of Andean cliffs
you forged a new star.

The sun declined too soon
for eyes that looked for

"the dove of cosmic peace."
But she will take wings
from the tight-clenched fists of Chile,
and out of the agony of Santiago
and out of your poetry,
Pablo Neruda.

Translated from the Slovak by Anča Vrbovská

HENRY BEISSEL

C'est la Mort

In Memoriam Pablo Neruda

1.

Hoist your black sails,
ship of fools,
you'll catch the protean monster
in the nets inside you.

They tore off the poet's head
and cast it singing into the sea
inside you singing ever since
seeing the shark and his kill
in a rhythm of waves
in the singing sea inside you.

2.

A bullet in the back of the neck,
then push the body over the cliff,
the fish won't mind
these white yellow brown red black bastards,
blood's all the same to them,
and water washes it off your hands.

But it's not the same to us
if anyone thinks that he can think
speak eat love dress differently—
he's the enemy! The difference is
what makes the difference. I can't wait
to get my hands on my hands on my
stones clubs spears bows knives guns.
To kill is to survive. Providence's on our side.
Come hell or high water. C'est la vie.
It's the next world that counts
right here and now.
                    Mind over matter.
They're poor because they're lazy.
They're sick because they don't wash.
They're starving because they never
they don't ever they're never ever—
you know . . . the trouble with all
those foreigners youngsters politicians is
they don't know what they don't know,
they don't have any respect for respect,
they don't follow their true Allah Baal Jesus,
their Krishna Moloch Buddha Osiris Jehova Zeus God—
wicked idolatrous infidel heathen heretics,
they've lost their souls to sin.
We must put them to the
consciousness of hate love torture
trial by water: if they drown they're innocent.
We're the elect. We save by strangling bless
by hanging. The kingdom of heaven
is for the weak is a drugtrip to slavedom is
nirvana for the poor in spirit for the rich
keep their heads well above water
is fleshdom for the strongest who survive.
The main thing is to get laid
                    in sacred ground.
That's what an education is for.
They got an education because they're rich,
they're rich because they got money,
they got money because they're
                    bloodsuckers

221

never get into hot water. Down
down with the down with the down with down!
We've got no use for the rich for the poor for people
thinking instead of doing not-thinking
what everybody else is not thinking doing.
If he's not for us
                    he's against us.
A blindfold and a firing squad: law and order.
The kids are innocent. Or maybe they're not.
The wife should've known. Still waters run
subversive. Screw her, let's all screw the
married to treason the whole bloody pack
gang mob platoon screw her
                                        from here
to eternity sperm runs
thicker than blood runs thicker than water.
There's never enough water
                                under the bridge.
Punch kick twist stab whip burn choke—
make him tell what we want him to tell,
stop him saying what we don't want to hear.
Suffering makes a man strong and wise.
Gouge out the eyes slice off ears and nose
tear out the tongue castrate disembowel draw
and quarter till the spirit is broken.
We've got no time for rebels and poets.
                                        Massacre
matter over mind.
                        Search and destroy the enemy
of the prophet of the god of the faith of the
leader of the state of the nation of the people
of the country of the city of the family of
everyone of us everywhere all over time and space.
It's out of this world, nuclear warfare is,
it really sends you bombs you missiles you
right out of this world, you and your friends
neighbours and relatives, all at one go,
that's the strategic advantage. You can't wash off
strontium 90 with soap and water. Those who don't

die right away just rot to the bone slowly,
at any rate the enemy will. C'est la vie.
We shall overcome. Everybody overcomes everybody else.
To the last man woman and child. Victory. Contra omnes.
There's no defeat. C'est la mort. All survivors are victors.
Victory or death—that's God's own sacred truth.

3.

Take it from me
thalassa
my eyes
thalassa O thalassa
my hands
wash
ash
O thalassa!

BERNARD KELLY

Tomorrow's Sun

for Pablo Neruda

who took down our eyes
wrote the thorns pressed
through a million streets
crackled with the exhausts of years
carboned his hands
on our cindered heads
saw sierras in tears
mountains in cages
who clanked from a generation's locks
unpicking the keyless multitude
saying notes through the bolts
a stream toppling
on fern sides

223

                    in his jacket pocket
              hills crammed with winds
                  under his shoes
            signaling bound cities
              to speak

        lifts icicled on office strings
              melting clothed drops
                  on desk lines
            skylines dreading
    hands tapping the nervous waves
                      of factories
              knees
        corners turned on advertisers
                  wrists
            yo-yoing throats
                      seized by manufactured
          waste
        the muffled no of millions
                  stifled
        chairmaned gags
                  bullioned on teeth
              fondling stocks and sures
        ears in safes
                  clamped to others vest sweat
            picking up through thickened fear
                  only the tap jag
        of forgetless
                  flesh hills
        eyes deposited   lensed steel
    helmeted against burst coronas
                  driven in averted   satchel smiles
              past world tornadoes   pavement futures
            who clocked   the speedometer bones
                  to cries
        suffocating other consciences
                  could inch his ears
      with grain   to skies   bottled in blood
              could plunge a hand
        in each torn human for tomorrow's sun

```
        he was our runner
                from womb bed
        to grave stone
                    he was
    his people's
            astronaut of birth
```

RAY SMITH

Neruda

Neruda, you turned from the sea,
turned toward the yellow flowers.
Neruda, the killers returned in the September of
    your death
to where Allende fell down alone defending Chile.
Neruda, now may your woodcutters awake
To burst a piñata of light above your cold small
        country.

BEATRIZ ALLENDE*

For the moment the fascists have achieved their goal of blocking the revolutionary process by assassinating the President and overthrowing the democratically elected government. They counted on military men, traitors to their country trained in U.S. military academies, on the financial backing of U.S. monopolies and on the political and diplomatic support of the United States government.

Today Chile, its soil stained by fascist boots, feels its institutions swept away, its culture destroyed, its progressive ideas persecuted, its finest sons tortured and murdered, its working-class districts and universities bombed—repressing the workers throughout the length of the nation.

*From a speech delivered in Cuba on September 8, 1973, by President Allende's daughter.

The fascists are mistaken, they have not won. Alongside the fascist brutality arises popular resistance which, taking its inspiration from the example of President Allende, is ready to fight and to win.

The Chilean people, today fighting in the streets, factories, hills and mines, call on the solidarity of all progressive people throughout the world, and especially the people of the United States.

We know that the imperialist U.S. government does not represent the real people of the U.S.A., and that in our fight we can count on them as did the Vietnamese. We can count on the solidarity of the workers, the national minorities, students, professionals, and other popular groupings which condemn the imperialist policy of the U.S. government, and which at the same time support the revolutionary process of those countries fighting for full sovereignty and social progress.

Appendix

Pablo Neruda: A Chronology

1904   Born June 12 in Parral, Chile, as Neftalí Ricardo Reyes, father a railroad engineer, mother a teacher.

1920   Publishes first poems and articles, under new name, Pablo Neruda, after Czech writer Jan Neruda.

1923–27   *Crepusculario*, first important poetry collection, followed by many other publications, poetry and prose (*Veinte poemas de amor, Canto para Bolívar*, etc.)

1927–35   Serves as Consul in Burma, Ceylon, Java, Singapore, Buenos Aires, Barcelona, Madrid.

1930   Marries Maria Antonieta Hagenaar.

1932   Publishes, in Chile, *Residencia en la Tierra* (between 1931–35).

1936   Publishes review: *The Poets of the World Defend the Spanish People* with Nancy Cunard in Paris. Separates from wife Maria Antonieta.

1938   Popular Front candidate, Pedro Aguirre Cerdo, a Radical, wins presidential election. Neruda travels through Chile helping in campaign. *España en el Corazón* published in Spain.

1939–40   Neruda named Consul for Loyalist Spain in Paris. Helps many Spanish refugees to escape from France to Chile. Later serves as Consul General in Mexico.

1945   Joins Communist Party of Chile. Elected Communist Senator. Receives the Chilean National Prize for Literature.

1948   Unseated as senator by Supreme Court and his arrest ordered because he is declared dangerous communist agitator. Flees the country.

1949   Member of World Peace Council. Visits Soviet Union, Poland, Hungary, and Mexico.

1950   *Canto General* is published. Visits Prague, Paris, Rome, India. Receives, together with Pablo Picasso and Paul Robeson the International Peace Prize for his poem *Que despierte el leñador* (Let the Railsplitter awake), part of *Canto General*.

1953	Receives Stalin Peace Prize.
1954	Publication of major works: *Odas Elementales, Alturas de Macchu Picchu*, and *Las Uvas y el Viento*.
1955	Marries Matilde Urrutia. Founds and directs review *La Gaceta de Chile*.
1958–68	Publishes about eight collections of new poems.
1962	Appointed academic member of the Faculty of Philosophy and Education of the University of Chile.
1964	Intensive work in the presidential election campaign for Allende.
1968	Is made member of the Chilean Academy of Languages. The Catholic University of Chile makes him Doctor Scientiae et Honoris Causa. Chilean Senate decorates him with the silver medal given to illustrious sons of Chile. In September 1968 he is designated presidential candidate for the Communist Party of Chile.
1970	Gives up his candidacy in favor of Allende as presidential candidate for the Unidad Popular, of which Communist Party is part. Supports Allende's campaign.
1971	Appointed Chilean Ambassador to France by Allende's government. In October receives Nobel Prize for Literature.
1973	Gives up ambassadorship for reasons of health. Goes to live in his house on Isla Negra. Publishes *Incitement to Nixonicide and Praise For the Chilean Revolution*. Dies September 23 in hospital in Santiago de Chile after illness aggravated by medical neglect and excitement and grief over events.

Some Dates in Chilean History

1540   The Spanish conquest of Chile.

1810   Chile joins the revolution against Spain.

1817   Chile wins its independence.

1851   Civil strife between owners and peasants, employers and workers, conservatives and liberals. Recurring in 1891 and 1907.

1881   With help of British, Chile defeats Peru and Bolivia and takes possession of the nitrate fields of the Atacama Desert.

1906   Luis Emilio Recabarren, founder of Chile's labor movement, is elected to Parliament but excluded from the Chamber of Deputies.

1911   Guggenheim interests pay $25 million to acquire the mine later famous as Chuquicamata, the largest open-pit copper mine in the world.

1912   Recabarren founds the Socialist Workers' Party.

1913   Bethlehem Steel Corporation obtains a 30-year concession to exploit Chile's iron ore deposits.

1914   The Andes Copper Mining Company, an Anaconda subsidiary, purchases La Africana copper mine.

1915   The Kennecott Copper Corporation, financed by the Morgan interests, expands its El Teniente Mine.

1918   The Liberal Alliance, Chile's first anti-oligarchic coalition, captures control of the lower house of Parliament.

1922   The Communist Party of Chile forms and later becomes the largest in Latin America.

1925   The constitution is passed, codifying Chile's break with the past. Church and state are separated. The constitution provides for direct taxation and some of the most advanced labor and welfare legislation in the world.

1929   The depression hits Chile hard. Sales of copper and nitrate decline disastrously. The depression brings great social unrest.

1931	The Communist Party is officially recognized, so that it can present candidates for local and national elections.
1933	The Socialist Party of Chile is founded, with strong support from the workers. It is a Marxist party and Salvador Allende is one of the founders.
1935–36	The Communist, Socialist and Radical parties unite for the first time in a Popular Front and work together against the oligarchic government of Alessandri.
1942	A Radical is elected president, with the support of the Communists and Socialists. Moderate reforms are accomplished.
1947	Communists receive 18% of the national vote in municipal elections, but shortly thereafter Communist ministers are dismissed and many are deported. Senator Pablo Neruda is unseated.
1948	The Communist Party is banned; many leaders are deported and jailed.
1949	Women are given the vote.
1952	The Chilean electorate chooses former dictator Carlos Ibañez, who promises to "sweep away" corruption. Allende is a presidential candidate for the first time, representing the People's Front.
1956	The Popular Action Front is formed, supporting a common slate against Ibañez.
1957	Anaconda invests $108 million more in Chilean mines.
1962	The first Agrarian Reform Bill is passed.
1965	Eduardo Frei, Christian Democrat, wins election against Allende.
1967	Nation-wide strike against government proposal to cut workers' salaries and temporarily prohibit the right to strike.
1969	The Massacre of Puerto Montt.
1970	*(Sept.)* As leader of a coalition of Communist, Socialist, and Radical parties, Allende is elected president.
1970	*(Oct.)* General Schneider, head of the armed forces, is assassinated in the first right-wing attack against the newly elected government.

1971   The Popular Unity Government, with unanimous support
       of Parliament, nationalizes the U.S.-owned copper com-
       panies which had extracted $4 billion in profits from
       Chile.

1973   *(Sept. 11)* Military coup overturns Allende government,
       assassinating the President and thousands more.

Other Books by Walter Lowenfels

Poetry

Episodes & Epistles
Finale of Seem
Apollinaire
Elegy for D. H. Lawrence
The Suicide
Sonnets of Love and Liberty
American Voices
Song of Peace
Some Deaths
Land of Roseberries
Found Poems
Translations from Scorpius
Thou Shalt Not Overkill

Editor

Walt Whitman's Civil War
Selections from Leaves of Grass
Poets of Today
Where is Vietnam?
New Jazz Poets
In the Time of Revolution
The Writing on the Wall
The Tenderest Lover
From the Belly of the Shark

Prose

To an Imaginary Daughter
Robert Grover's The Portable Walter
The Poetry of My Politics
The Life of Fraenkel's Death
The Revolution Is to Be Human
Reality Prime

Acknowledgments

This book has been a cooperative enterprise. Dozens of people, publications, and organizations throughout the world helped to gather and select the contents. I mention here only a few: Nan Braymer, whose judgment and all-around editorial help was invaluable; Lillian Lowenfels, Lenore Veltfort, Ruth Lisa Schechter, Charles Hayes, Dick Lourie, Joseph Bruchac, Henry Beissel, Charles Dobzynski, Fred Cogswell, Marc Plourde, Bob Honig, P.E.N., Center for Cuban Studies, and, above all, the translators.

Walter Lowenfels

Etel Adnan, "A Candle for Pablo Neruda," published by permission of Etel Adnan. Rafael Alberti, "With Pablo Neruda in My Heart," from *Casa de las Américas*, No. 83, published by permission of the Center for Cuban Studies. Yusuf Al-Khal, "For Neruda Upon His Death," published by permission of Yusuf Al-Khal. Beatrice Allende, statement from *What Happened in Chile*, reprinted by permission of the Venceremos Brigade. Salvador Allende, "Farewell Speech over Radio Magallenes, September 11, 1973," published by permission of the Common Front For Latin America (COFFLA). George Amabile, "Canto," published by permission of George Amabile. A. Appercelle, "To Chile—To Allende—," published by permission of A. Appercelle. Aragon, "Élégie à Pablo Neruda," published by permission of Aragon. Luis Cardoza y Aragón, "Pablo Neruda," published by permission of Luis Cardoza y Aragón. Bob Arnold, "Faraway, Like The Deer's Eye," published by permission of Bob Arnold. Miguel Angel Asturias, "Pablo Neruda Alive," published by permission of *Revista Crisis*, Buenos Aires.

Eva Bán, "In Memorium Pablo Neruda," published by permission of Eva Ban. Sharon Barba, "For Pablo Neruda," Copyright © 1974 by *The Painted Bride Quarterly, Inc.* John Barnes, article reprinted by permission of *Newsweek*. Copyright Newsweek, Inc., 1973. Willis Barnstone, "Pablo Neruda," published by permission of Willis Barnstone. Nelson Estupiñan Bass, "A Candle for Pablo," published by permission of Nelson Estupiñan Bass. Lee Baxandall, "Neruda's Last Poem," published by permission of Lee Baxandall. Henry Beissel, "C'est la Mort," is part 11 of a long poem "Rhythm of Waves" from *The Salt I Taste* by Henry Beissel (Montreal, 1974), reprinted by permission of Henry Beissel. Tobias Berggren, "Poem from Gotland, September 1973," published by permission of Tobias Berggren. Zoe Best, "Neruda," published by permission of Zöe Best. Alain Bosquet, "Tract For General Pinochet," published by permission of Alain Bosquet. Volker Braun, "Last Residence on Earth," published by permission of *Action Poetique*. Jean Brierre, "Me Duele Chile," published by permission of Jean Brierre. Alan Britt, "Pablo Neruda's Death," reprinted from *UT Review*, by permission of Alan Britt. Joseph Bruchac, "Pine Cone," published by permission of Joseph Bruchac.

Miguel Cabezas, "Victor Jara Died Singing," reprinted from *University Review* (June 1974) by permission of Walter Lowenfels. Olga Cabral, "Poem About Death," published by permission of Olga Cabral. Michel Cahour, "Now the night falls on Santiago," published by permission of *Action Poetique*. Charles Cantrell, "The Unbound Voice," published by permission of Charles Cantrell. Primo Castrillo, "Pablo Neruda," from *Zampoñas Teluricas* (Ed. Juan Ponce de Leon, Palencia de Castilla, Spain, 1974), published by permission of Primo Castrillo. Syl Cheney Coker, "On the Death of Pablo Neruda," published by permission of Syl Cheney Coker. Neeli Cherry, "For Neruda, For Chile," published by permission of Neeli Cherry. Chinweizu, "The Return of the Flies," published by permission of Chinweizu. John Robert Colombo, "Proverbial Neruda," Copyright © 1975 by J. R. Colombo. Jack Curtis, "The House," published by permission of Jack Curtis.

Margot de Silva, "Don Pablo Neruda," published by permission of Margot de Silva. W. S. Di Piero, "Morning in Santiago," published by permission of W. S. Di Piero. Mike Dobbie, "you fell from the skies/the last days," published by permission of Mike Dobbie. Franz Douskey, "Amorphous Water," published by permission of Franz Douskey. Ann duCille, "For your preservation," published by permission of Ann duCille.

Ronald Lee Emmons, "For Our Brothers in Chile," from his forthcoming book *Exiles in Babylon* (Third World Press, Chicago, 1975), published by permission of Ronald Lee Emmons. Eduardo Escobar, "Goodbye to Neruda Without Raising My Hand," published by permission of Eduardo Escobar. Gary Esolen, "Dialectic: To the Victims of History," published by permission of Gary Esolen.

Rudolf Fabry, "What About It, Brother World?" published by permission of Rudolf Fabry. Jose-Angel Figueroa, "Pablo Neruda," from *Boricua* by José-Angel Figueroa, Copyright © 1974, published by permission of José-Angel Figueroa.

Pierre Gamarra, "Ballad of Chilean Liberty," published by permission of *Action Poetique*. Louise Gareau-Des-Bois, "Dream of the Other America," published by permission of Louise Gareau-Des-Bois. Ricardo Garibay, "Pablo Neruda's Funeral," reprinted from *Excelsior* (Mexico City), by permission of Ricardo Garibay. Serge Gavronsky, "what was written in black," published by permission of Serge Gavronsky. Allen Ginsberg, "To a Dead Poet," reprinted from *P.E.N. Club Magazine*, by permission of Allen Ginsberg. Michael Gizzi, "For & After Pablo Neruda," reprinted from *Carmela Bianca* by Michael Gizzi (Bone Whistle Press, 1974), by permission of Michael Gizzi. Carlos Golibart, "For Pablo Neruda," published by permission of Carlos Golibart. Darcy Gottlieb, "Come, Neruda, Come," reprinted from *No Witness But Ourselves* by Darcy Gottlieb, by permission of Darcy Gottlieb and the University of Missouri Press. Copyright 1973 by Darcy Gottlieb. Ida Gramcko, "To Neruda Incommunicado," published by permission of Ida Gramcko. Dominique Grandmont, "An Example," published by permission of *Action Poetique*. Susan Grathwohl, "For Pablo Neruda," published by permission of Susan Grathwohl. Steven Michael Gray, "Return of Son of La Guardia," published by permission of Steven Michael Gray. Eric Greinke, "The Diplomat," published by permission of Eric Greinke. Eamon Grennan, "The Chilean Singer," published by permission of Eamon Grennan. Sean Griffin, ". . . And Gather the Banners," published by permission of Sean Griffin. Nicolás Guillen, "To Chile," from *Casa de las Américas*, No. 83, published by permission of the Center for Cuban Studies.

Mathilde Urrutia Neruda, "Neruda's Last Days," reprinted by permission of *The Daily World.*

Ed Ochester, "For Neruda," published by permission of Ed Ochester. Tanure Ojaide, "Chicho" published by permission of Tanure Ojaide. Kemal Ozer, "If Chile Is Bent Like a Dagger," published by permission of Kemal Özer. Orlin Orlinov, "Chilean Fiesta," published by permission of Sophy Todorchev. Emily Paine, "For the Spirit of Neruda," published by permission of Emily Paine.

Cecil Rajendra, "For Pablo Neruda," published by permission of Cecil Rajendra. David Ray, "The Andes," published by permission of David Ray. Lionel Ray, ". . . it was from far away under the lantern that the shadows wiped out the dignity of questions . . ." published by permission of *Action Poetique.* Ishmael Reed, "Poem Delivered Before Assembly of Colored People At Glide Memorial Church, Oct. 4, 1973 And Called To Protest Recent Events In The Sovereign Republic Of Chile," published by permission of Ishmael Reed, Copyright © 1974 by Ishmael Reed. Robert Reinhold, "On the Passing of Neruda," published by permission of Robert Reinhold. Christian Riondet, "Words For Pablo," published by permission of Christian Riondet. Geoffrey Rips, "Resurrection: For Allende," published by permission of Geoffrey Rips. Giannis Ritsos, "Chile," published by permission of Jack Lindsay. Maria Rival, "when he died," published by permission of Maria Rival. José Rodeiro, "The Cube-Root of Pablo," published by permission of José Rodeiro. Leo Romero, "For Pablo Neruda," published by permission of Leo Romero. Robert Rosenberg, "To the Memory of Pablo Neruda," published by permission of Robert Rosenberg. Muriel Rukeyser, "Neruda, The Wine," published by permission of Muriel Rukeyser.

Andrew Salkey, "Victor," published by permission of Andrew Salkey. Piero Santi, "For Chile—Love," published by permission of Piero Santi. Ruth Lisa Schechter, "Are We Saying All Your Verses?" reprinted from *Offshore* by Ruth Lisa Schechter (Barlenmir House, 1974), by permission of Ruth Lisa Schechter. Tom Schmidt, "Vagando," published by permission of Tom Schmidt. James R. Scrimgeour, "Spotted off the Coast of Chile September 1973," published by permission of James R. Scrimgeour. James Scully, "Now Sing," published by permission of James Scully. James Scully, "Toque de Queda," published by permission of James Scully. Nina Serrano, "Elegy for Pablo Neruda," published by permission of Nina Serrano. Jory Sherman, "Poema Para Pablo Neruda," published by permission of Jory Sherman. Ray Smith, "Neruda," reprinted from *North Country Anvil* (No. 8, Oct.-Nov. 1973) by permission of Ray Smith and *North Country Anvil.* György Somlyó, " 'Chile, when shall. . . .' " published by permission of György Somlyó. Hugo Stanchi, "A Trilogy in Memory of Pablo Neruda," published by permission of Hugo Stanchi. Nico Suarez, "To Pablo Neruda," published by permission of Nico Suarez. Michael Szporer, "elegy for allende," published by permission of Michael Szporer.

John Tagliabue, "The Self Not Seen," published by permission of John Tagliabue. Nathaniel Tarn, "At Gloucester, Mass., After Foreign Travel," published by permission of Nathaniel Tarn, Copyright © 1974 by Nathaniel Tarn. Lorenzo Thomas, "Suicide Administration," published by permission of Lorenzo Thomas. Carol Tinker, " 'Another Defenestration in Prague,' " published by permission of Carol Tinker. Quincy Troupe, "These Crossings, These Words," reprinted from *Sunbury* (Vol. 1, No. 1, Virginia Scott, Editor), will be published in *Ash Doors And Juju Guitars* by Quincy Troupe (Random House, 1975), published by permission of Quincy Troupe. Osman Turkay, "Doomsday in Santiago," published by permission of Osman Türkay.

Karl Vennberg, "First day of autumn 1973," published by permission of Karl Vennberg. Pedro Vera, "Chile, the wretched beasts," from *Casa de las Américas*, No. 83, published by permission of the Center for Cuban Studies and Pedro Vera. William Wantling, "Alive, Alive," published by permission of William Wantling. Tom Wayman, "The Return," published by permission of Tom Wayman. Tom Wayman, "the chilean elegies," reprinted from *kayak* by permission of Tom Wayman. Ramona Weeks, "For Neruda," reprinted from *Squeezebox* (Vol. I, No. 2, 1974), by permission of Ramona Weeks. Clarke Wells, "for pablo neruda 1904–1973," published by permission of Clarke Wells. Elena Wilkinson, "Chile: Elegia de la Venganza," published by permission of Elena Wilkinson.

Evgenii Yevtushenko, "The Generals' Boots," published by permission of *Action Poetique* and the Copyright Agency of the U.S.S.R. Robert Zaller, "Lament for Neftalí Reyes," published by permission of Robert Zaller. Harriet Zinnes, "For Pablo Neruda," published by permission of Harriet Zinnes.

CONTENTS

Rudolf Fabry	What About It, Brother World	iii
Walter Lowenfels	From the Editor	vii
Hortensia Bussi de Allende		*ix*

I. Grief Is a Large Space

Margot de Silva	Don Pablo Neruda	3
Eva Bán	In Memoriam Pablo Neruda	4
Aragon	Élégie à Pablo Neruda	5
John Tagliabue	The Self Not Seen	7
Miguel Angel Asturias	Pablo Neruda Alive	8
Ramona Weeks	For Neruda	9
Michael Gizzi	For & After Pablo Neruda	10
Rafael Alberti	With Pablo Neruda in My Heart	11
David Ray	The Andes	13
Jean Brierre	Me Duele Chile	14
Leo Romero	For Pablo Neruda	16
Emily Paine	For the Spirit of Neruda	17
Volker Braun	Last Residence On Earth	18
Rafael Mendoza	This Pablo	19
Muriel Rukeyser	Neruda, The Wine	20

II. Light That Arrives

Matilde Urrutia Neruda	Pablo's Death	23
José H. Llubien	Neruda: Light That Arrives	24
Ruth Lisa Schechter	Are We Saying All Your Verses?	26
Jack Curtis	The House	27

Thomas McGrath	A Warrant for Pablo Neruda	28
Joseph Bruchac	Pine Cone	29
Yusuf Al-Khal	For Neruda Upon His Death	31
Primo Castrillo	Pablo Neruda	32
Robert Rosenberg	To the Memory of Pablo Neruda	33
Allen Ginsberg	To a Dead Poet	34
Robert Zaller	Lament for Neftalí Reyes	35
Hugo Stanchi	A trilogy in memory of Pablo Neruda	35
Ed Ochester	For Neruda	38
Duane Locke	Kaivalya	39
Ida Gramcko	To Neruda Incommunicado	40

III. Blues for Salvador

Salvador Allende	Farewell Speech over Radio Magallenes, September 11, 1973	45
Karl Vennberg	First Day of Autumn 1973	47
Geoffrey Rips	Resurrection: For Allende	48
Michael Szporer	elegy for allende	48
Tanure Ojaide	Chicho	49
A. Appercelle	To Chile—To Allende—	50
D. H. Melhem	Homage to Allende	51
Tobias Berggren	Poem From Gotland, September 1973	52
Gayl Jones	Más Allá	54
Gary Esolen	Dialectic: To the Victims of History	55
Antar Sudan Katara Mberi	Blues for Salvador	56
Lee Baxandall	Neruda's Last Poem	57

IV. Tract for General Pinochet

John Barnes		61
Alain Bosquet	Tract For General Pinochet	62
Tom Wayman	The Return	63
Gilbert Langevin	Anti-Cancer Concert	65
Christina Morris	Memo	66
Elena Wilkinson	*Chile: Elegía de la Venganza*	67
Carol Tinker	"Another Defenestration in Prague"	68
Nelson Estupiñan Bass	A Candle for Pablo	69
Piero Santi	For Chile—Love	71
Harvey Mudd	The Near Sierra	73
Louise Gareau-Des-Bois	Dream of the Other America	74
Pedro Vera	Chile, the wretched beasts . . .	75

V. The Chilean Singer

Miguel Cabezas	Victor Jara Died Singing	79
James Scully	Now Sing	81
Eamon Grennan	The Chilean Singer	81
Linda Lizut	Untitled	83
June Jordan	Poem: To my sister . . .	84
Bob Arnold	Faraway, Like The Deer's Eye	86
Andrew Salkey	Victor	87
Hugo Loyácono	Victor Jara	88
Victor Jara	Chile Stadium	89

VI. Bloodying the Twilight

Ricardo Garibay	Pablo Neruda's Funeral	93
Carlos Golibart	For Pablo Neruda	94
Christian Riondet	Words for Pablo	96
Serge Gavronsky	what was written in black	99

Lionel Ray   . . . it was from far away
under the lantern that the
shadows wiped out the
dignity of questions . . .   100

Pierre Gamarra   Ballad of Chilean Liberty   101

Hans Juergensen   Pablo Neruda   102

Quincy Troupe   These Crossings, These Words   103

Neeli Cherry   For Neruda, For Chile   105

Nícolas Guillen   To Chile   106

James Scully   Toque de Queda   107

Bob Honig   Did you ask for me?   108

Michel Cahour   Now the night falls on
Santiago   111

Zöe Best   Neruda   112

VII.   Alive, Alive

William Wantling   Alive, Alive   115

Willis Barnstone   Pablo Neruda   115

Cecil Rajendra   For Pablo Neruda   117

Alan Britt   Pablo Neruda's Death   118

Pat Lowther   Anniversary Letter to Pablo   120

Charle Hayes   Pablo   121

Syl Cheney Coker   On the Death of Pablo Neruda   124

Lorenzo Thomas   Suicide Administration   126

José-Angel Figueroa   pablo neruda   127

Will Inman   Late Chant for Pablo Neruda   128

Robert Reinhold   On the Passing of Neruda   128

Luis Cardoza y Aragón   Pablo Neruda   130

Steve Kowit   "Neruda's remains were
expelled this week . . ."   131

VIII. Doomsday in Santiago

Osman Türkay	Doomsday in Santiago	137
Eva Kovácová	What's Theirs	138
Elias Hruska-Cortes	*El Golpe*	139
Mike Dobbie	you fell from the skies/the last days	143
Stuart McCarrell	For Chile	145
Kyoko Komori	Driving Nails with a Rock	146
Alejandro Murguia	Newsreport	148
José Kozer	Death Is Pitiless	149
Kemal Özer	If Chile Is Bent Like a Dagger	150
György Somlyó	"Chile, when shall . . ."	150

IX. One Circle of Light

Olga Cabral	Poem About Death	155
Ishmael Reed	Poem Delivered Before Assembly Of Colored People Held At Glide Memorial Church, Oct. 4, 1973 And Called To Protest Recent Events In The Sovereign Republic Of Chile	156
Anselm Hollo	Epitafio	159
Tom Wayman	the chilean elegies	160
Thomas McGrath	Lament for Pablo Neruda	161
Nina Serrano	Elegy for Pablo Neruda	162
Maria Rival	when he died	163
Stephen Kessler	Beyond Everything	165
Nico Suarez	To Pablo Neruda	166
Etel Adnan	A Candle for Pablo Neruda	169
John Robert Colombo	Proverbial Neruda	170
William Harrold	Musical Water	171
Eric Greinke	The Diplomat	171

X.   The Sky Is Red

Dominique Grandmont	An Example	175
W. S. Di Piero	Morning in Santiago	176
Clarke Wells	for pablo neruda 1904–1973	177
James R. Scrimgeour	Spotted off the Coast of Chile September 1973	178
Evgenii Yevtushenko	The Generals' Boots	178
L. M. Jendrzejczyk	Migration	180
Ronald Lee Emmons	For Our Brothers in Chile	181
Charles Cantrell	The Unbound Voice	182
Harriet Zinnes	For Pablo Neruda	183
Orlin Orlinov	Chilean Fiesta	184

XI.   Canto

George Amabile	Canto	187
Steven Michael Gray	Return of Son of La Guardia	188
Jory Sherman	Poema Para Pablo Neruda	190
Chinweizu	The Return of the Flies	191
Sean Griffin	. . . And Gather the Banners	192
Giannis Ritsos	Chile	193
Robert Hass	Elegy: Residence on Earth	194
Dick Lourie	today	195
Tom Schmidt	Vagando	196

XII.   Tomorrow's Sun

Walter Lowenfels	For Pablo Neruda	201
Nathaniel Tarn	At Gloucester, Mass., After Foreign Travel	201
Sharon Barba	For Pablo Neruda	204
José Rodeiro	The Cube-Root of Pablo	205

Vincius de Moraes	Natural History of Pablo Neruda	206
David Martinson	South Wind in October	208
Ann du Cille	For Your Preservation	209
Eduardo Escobar	Goodbye to Neruda Without Raising My Hand	210
Franz Douskey	Amorphous Water	213
Edwin Honig	Pablo Neruda	214
Darcy Gottlieb	Come, Neruda, Come	215
Barbara A. Holland	The Insane Pursuit of Tío Pablo	216
Susan Grathwohl	For Pablo Neruda	217
Gabriela Haringova	For Pablo Neruda	219
Henry Beissel	C'est la Mort	220
Bernard Kelly	Tomorrow's Sun	223
Ray Smith	Neruda	225
Beatriz Allende		225

Appendix

Pablo Neruda: A Chronology	229
Some Dates in Chilean History	231
Other Books by Walter Lowenfels	235
Acknowledgments	237
Contents	243